Carlos L. Garri

The Purity Fetish and the Crisis of Western Marxism

© Midwestern Marx Publishing Press

The Publishing Press of
THE MIDWESTERN MARX INSTITUTE FOR MARXIST
THEORY AND POLITICAL ANALYSIS

Spring, 2023

www.midwesternmarx.com

Dubuque, IA/ Carbondale, IL USA

ISBN: 978-0-578-27836-0 (paperback)

ISBN: 979-8-218-95191-7 (eBook)

Midwestern Marx Publishing Press
Titles Published

1. Thomas Riggins. *Reading the Classical Texts of Marxism*, 2022.
2. Carlos L. Garrido. *Marxism and the Dialectical Materialist Worldview: An Anthology of Classical Marxist Texts on Dialectical Materialism*, 2022.
3. Thomas Riggins. *Eurocommunism: A Critical Reading of Santiago Carrillo and Eurocommunist Revisionism*, 2022.
4. Carlos Martinez. *No Great Wall: On the Continuities of the Chinese Revolution*, 2022.

Some Forthcoming Titles

1. Carlos L. Garrido and Noah Khrachvik. *Selected Works of Henry Winston*.
2. Thomas Riggins. *Christopher Caudwell and His Critics: A Study of Caudwell's Philosophy of Art and its Critical Responses*.
3. Edward Liger Smith. *What About Venezuela?: How Socialism Worked in Venezuela and Why the US Needs it Too*.
4. Yanis Iqbal. *Education in the Age of Neoliberal Dystopia*.
5. Noah Khrachvik. *What is to be Done... Like Now?*
6. Gabriel Rockhill, William Robinson, Salvador Rangel, Jennifer Ponce de León, Carlos Martinez, Carlos L. Garrido, Edward Smith, Noah Khrachvik, Thomas Riggins, Hilbourne Watson, et. al. *Against the Fake Left: Marxist Critiques of Contemporary Radicalisms*.

Endorsements

"This is a very important new work from Carlos Garrido. Here he explains in full detail the "purity fetish," which has afflicted and hobbled the Western left for too long. Not only does the purity fetish prevent the Western Left from understanding the century or more of actual socialist construction in many parts of the world, but it also prevents this very same Left from appreciating and drawing insight from the history of genuine socialist struggles in their own countries. This book will soon become a must-read for anyone who is serious about the socialist road and the goal of communism."

- **Roland Boer**, professor at Renmin University of China, Beijing. Author of many books, including *Socialism with Chinese Characteristics: A Guide for Foreigners* (2021), *Friedrich Engels and the Foundations of Socialist Governance* (2021), and *Socialism in Power: On the History and Theory of Socialist Governance* (2023).

"This book is a healthy antidote to the widespread infantile leftism that infects the American left. As Lenin pointed out in *Left-Wing Communism: An Infantile Disorder*, those so called Marxists who are so wrapped up in their one sided views that they can't work with others, whether it's right-wing deviationism towards the bourgeois parties (the Democratic Party as an ally!) or complete ultra-left rejection of bourgeois coalitions (our way or the highway), such thinking retards the revolutionary movement to overthrow the capitalist system. This book will help such comrades to grow up and learn how to apply the dialectical method to these issues."

- **Thomas Riggins**, retired philosophy teacher (NYU, The New School, and others), former associate editor at Political Affairs, Chief Editorial Counselor at the Midwestern Marx Institute and author of *Reading the Classical Texts of Marxism* (2022) and *Eurocommunism: A Critical Reading* (2022).

"Unlike Athena, socialism does not spring forth, fully formed from the head of a god or, by extension, the minds of people. It emerges in the here and now through a dialectical and contradictory process of real-world social transformation. This is precisely what Carlos Garrido astutely argues in this timely and provocative book: we need to embrace *the dialectics of socialism* as an antidote to the purity fetish that plagues the Western Left, pinning it into a position of controlled counter-hegemony. This book—a clarion call for the collective project of building socialism—should be widely read and discussed!"

- **Gabriel Rockhill**, Founding Director of the Critical Theory Workshop / Atelier de Théorie Critique & Professor of Philosophy at Villanova University. Author of many books, including *Counter-History of the Present: Untimely Interrogations* into *Globalization, Technology, and Democracy* (2017) and *Interventions in Contemporary Thought: History, Politics, Aesthetics* (2016).

"The Western Left has a sordid history of complicity with "fascist falsifiers," as Georgi Dimitrov noted in 1935, who scurrilously distort the revolutionary gains achieved in the socialist states and mount counter-revolutionary attacks aimed at extinguishing the emancipatory sparks of actually existing socialism. In adroitly dissecting the philosophical underpinnings of what passes for Marxism in the academy – a pseudo-radical pedagogy that has misled generations of students and inhibited the development of revolutionary political praxis in Western societies – Carlos Garrido demonstrates the importance of theoretical education in dialectical materialism for the class struggle in the contemporary conjuncture."

- **Helmut-Harry Loewen**, a veteran anti-apartheid and anti-fascist campaigner in Western Canada, is an associate of the Institute for the Humanities at Simon Fraser University and a retired University of Winnipeg lecturer in sociology and criminological theory.

"In *The Purity Fetish and the Crisis of Western Marxism*, Carlos Garrido seriously examines the dogmatism and eurocentrism that have had such a toxic influence on the development of the Western left. Crucially, the book addresses the failure of so many Marxists to understand actually existing socialism; their seeming inability to understand movements with different cultural and philosophical roots to those of the European working class of the 19th century.

This is not simply an academic question. The socialist countries - most prominently China - are leading the way towards a new future for humanity; the type of future where we can prevent climate catastrophe, avert nuclear war, and build what Xi Jinping refers to as a community with a shared future for mankind. These countries are blazing the way to a life beyond capitalism, and for that exact reason they're being subjected to an escalating hybrid warfare by the US and its allies.

Carlos Garrido's book is a valuable tool in the struggle to build a symbiotic relationship of solidarity, comradeship, respect and mutual learning between the Western left and the socialist world."

- **Carlos Martinez** is an independent researcher and political activist from London, Britain. He is the co-founder of No Cold War and Friends of Socialist China, and the author of *The End of the Beginning: Lessons of the Soviet Collapse* (2019) and *No Great Wall: On the Continuities of the Chinese Revolution* (2022).

"As the gap between conditions that cry out for socialist transformation and the long-diminishing political capacities of the Western left grows ever more dangerous, Garrido's brilliantly pithy and well-thought philosophical book argues that a good part of this gap is accounted for by the Western and US left's 'purity fetish.'

This fetish, Garrido argues, drawing from Hegel, Marx, Parenti and Losurdo, arises from an inability to think dialectically, an inability to realize that the abstract has no existence other than in necessarily compromised concrete instances that are always and everywhere 'desecrated by the meanness of reality.'

Garrido's accessible philosophical discussion is indispensable for understanding much of the Western left's inability to think dialectically, to truly follow Hegel and Marx rather than just invoke them, to understand the struggle for socialism as it is, rather than as it might be in the politically juvenile imaginations of so many.

Garrido's punchy discourse deals both with the reality of building socialism in China and with the difficulties of building socialism in the US. His demands that black liberation movements connect up with the US's revolutionary traditions will inevitably arouse debate, but it is likely one that must be had."

- **Radhika Desai**, Professor at the Department of Political Studies and Director of the Geopolitical Economy Research Group at University of Manitoba, Winnipeg, Canada. Some of her recent books include *Geopolitical Economy: After US Hegemony, Globalization and Empire* (2013), *Karl Polanyi and Twenty First Century Capitalism* (2020), *Revolutions* (2020), *Japan's Secular Stagnation* (2022), and *Capitalism, Coronavirus and War: A Geopolitical Economy* (2022). With Alan Freeman, she co-edits the Geopolitical Economy book series with Manchester University Press and the Future of Capitalism book series with Pluto Press.

Acknowledgements and Dedications

This book would not have been possible without the *Midwestern Marx Institute for Marxist Theory and Political Analysis*, specifically, without the plethora of conversations I have had with Edward Liger Smith, Thomas Riggins, and Noah Khrachvik over the years. I am also greatly indebted with the discussions and collaborations I have had with friends, comrades, and colleagues like Gabriel Rockhill, Mitchell K. Jones, Calla Winchell, Radhika Desai, Alan Freeman, Jean-Pierre Reed, Alfred Frankowski, Alex Zambito, Ramiro Sebastián Fúnez, Carlos Martinez, Paul So, Vijay Prashad and many others. I am also especially grateful to my wife and parents; without whose support this book would have also not been possible. I would like to dedicate this book to my newborn son, Lucian Thomas Garrido, to the readers and watchers of the *Midwestern Marx Institute*, and to the younger generations facing what seems to be a futureless future as this world based on exploitation, oppression, and looting crumbles right before their very eyes. For this book I share the sentiment Lenin expressed in the end of his first major publication in 1899, *The Development of Capitalism in Russia*, "if the writer of these lines has succeeded in providing some material for clarifying these problems, he may regard his labors as not having been fruitless."

Table of Contents

Introduction

Western Marxism[1] suffers from the same problem as F. Scott Fitzgerald's Jay Gatsby in the novel *The Great Gatsby* – each has a fixation on perfection and purity that leaves perpetually unfulfilled all that it claims to desire. Jay seeks a return to the purity of his first encounter with Daisy, and in the impossibility of this return to purity, the actual potential for a relationship is lost. Western Marxists seek a pure form of socialism, a pure proletariat, a pure national-historical past, but in the impossibility of such a purity arising, they lose the potential to actualize or defend any socialist revolution. The purity of each is met with the fact that reality itself is never pure – it always contains negations, imperfections, and impurities.

Jay Gatsby cannot officially reestablish himself with Daisy insofar as she admits to having loved Tom Buchanan – her husband – during the intermediate time before she re-connects with Jay. This imperfection, this negation of purity, is unacceptable – Daisy must tell Tom she never loved him to reestablish the purity of their first encounter. With no purity, there can be no relationship.

Similarly, for Western Marxists the triumphant socialist experiments of the 20th and 21st century, in their mistakes and 'totalitarianisms,' desecrate the purity in the holiness of their conception of socialism. The USSR must be rejected, the Spanish civil war upheld; Cuban socialism must be condemned, but the 1959 revolution praised; Allende and Sankara are idols, Fidel and Kim Il-Sung tyrants, etc. What has died in purity can be supported, what has had to grapple with the mistakes and pressures that arise out of the complexities and contradictions of building socialism in the imperialist phase of capitalism, that must be condemned.

---

[1] By Western Marxism I am referring specifically to a broad current in Marxism that comes about a quarter into the last century as a rejection of the Soviet Union and Marxism-Leninism. It is today the dominant form of 'Marxism' in Western academia. It encapsulates everything from the Frankfurt school, the French Marxists of the 60s-70s, the New Left, and the forms of Marxism Humanism that arise alongside these. Often, they phrase their projects as a Marxism that 'returns to its Hegelian roots,' centering the Marx of the *Economic and Philosophical Manuscripts of 1844* and reading the mature Marx only in light of the projects of the younger Marx. Some of the main theorists today include Jürgen Habermas, Slavoj Žižek, Alain Badiou, Kevin Anderson etc. Although it might be tempting to just refer to this block as 'Non-Marxist-Leninist Marxists,' I would urge against doing so, for there are many Marxist currents in the global South which, although drinking from the fountain of Marxism-Leninism, do not explicitly consider themselves Marxist-Leninists and yet do not have the same "purity fetish" outlook that Western Marxists do.

As was diagnosed by Brazilian communist Jones Manoel's essay, "Western Marxism Loves Purity and Martyrdom, But Not Real Revolution," Western Marxism's fetishization of purity, failures, and resistance as an end in itself creates "a kind of narcissistic orgasm of defeat and purity."[2] Manoel rightly points out the fact that Western "Marxism preserves the purity of theory to the detriment of the fact that it has never produced a revolution anywhere on the face of the Earth."[3] Western Marxists celebrate the emergence of a revolutionary movement; but, when this revolutionary movement is triumphant in taking power, and hence faced with making the difficult decisions the concrete reality of imperialism, a national bourgeoisie, economic backwardness, etc. force upon it, the Western Marxists flee with shouts of betrayal! For the Western Marxists, all practical deviation from their purity is seen as a betrayal of the revolution, and thus, the cries of 'state capitalism' and 'authoritarianism' emerge.

Manoel, reflecting on the work of the late Domenico Losurdo's *Western Marxism*, does a superb job in concisely elaborating on the thesis brought forth in Losurdo's text. Nonetheless, he (as well as Losurdo) conceives of this theoretical lapse as being "smuggled in as contraband from Christianity."[4] The ideological grounds for Western Marxism, then, are "rooted in the Judeo-Christian tradition," as Losurdo argues.[5] In this work, I will begin by arguing that although Christian mysticism may be present, the root of the rot is not Christian contraband, but Western metaphysics (which precedes Christian mysticism itself). The root, in essence, is found in the fixated categories that have permeated Western philosophy; in the general conception that Truth is in the unchanging, in the permanent, in substance; and only indirectly in the mystical forms these have taken under the Christian tradition. The diagnosis Engels gave reductive Marxists in 1890 applies to today's Western Marxists – "what all these gentlemen lack is dialectics."[6]

However, I wish to expand beyond Losurdo's analysis in other ways as well. For one, I will develop the integrative concept of the *purity fetish* as

[2] Jones Manoel, "Western Marxism Loves Purity and Martyrdom, But Not Real Revolution," *Black Agenda Report* (June 10, 2020): https://blackagendareport.com/western-marxism-loves-purity-and-martyrdom-not-real-revolution
[3] Jones Manoel, "Western Marxism Loves Purity and Martyrdom, But Not Real Revolution."
[4] Jones Manoel, "Western Marxism Loves Purity and Martyrdom, But Not Real Revolution."
[5] Domenico Losurdo, *Western Marxism* (Madrid: Trotta, 2019), 178.
[6] Karl Marx and Friedrich Engels, *Marx-Engels Collected Works (MECW) Vol. 49* (New York: International Publishers, 2001), 87.

the notion which dialectically captures the variety of ways this obsession with purity manifests itself in Western Marxists (and US Marxists in particular). The purity fetish, I will argue, is an integral component of the Western metaphysical outlook, an outlook which concretizes itself in a variety of ways throughout history, but which sustains, with very few exceptions, key philosophical assumptions traceable to Parmenidean metaphysics. In the US left this can be found in three major areas, all of which prevent both the acquisition of truth and the development of a socialist movement: 1) in the assessment of socialist (and non-socialist but anti-imperialist) struggles abroad, where the phenomenon Max Scheler (elaborated from Nietzsche) calls *ressentiment* is indubitably present; 2) in the assessment of the diverse character of the working class at home; and 3) in their *national nihilistic* assessment of US history. In each of these areas, the purity fetish limits their judgment to being at best one-sided and fetters their practical efforts to develop the subjective factor in the working masses.[7]

The Marxist variation of the purity fetish worldview, however, did not spontaneously emerge out of a void. It is grounded on objective forces, on a "political economy of knowledge" which has propelled what Gabriel Rockhill calls "the global theory industry."[8] It is also, as theorists like Barbara and John Ehrenreach, Catherine Liu, Gus Hall, Noah Khrachvik and others have noted, grounded on class positions outside of the working class, and within petty-bourgeois and/or professional-managerial class (PMC) positions. These class positions, which we may classify under the broader term of 'middle class,' are intermeshed in the culture and institutions of what has been called "the Iron Triangle of academia, media, and NGOs."[9] Out of this culture also stems a distinctive mode of socialist identification which, under the conditions Hans Georg Moeller and Paul D'Ambrosio have labeled as *profilicity*, reduces what being a socialist is to a counter-cultural identity, or profile, that is more concerned with its preservation, than with achieving political power.

Taking these objective and subjective conditions into consideration, what can help overcome Western Marxism's purity fetish is not simply, as

---

[7] An elaboration of the objective/subjective factor distinction can be found at the beginning of the fourth chapter of this book.
[8] Gabriel Rockhill, "The CIA and the Frankfurt School's Anti-Communism," *The Philosophical Salon* (June 27, 2022): https://thephilosophicalsalon.com/the-cia-the-frankfurt-schools-anti-communism/
[9] Class Unity, "The Left's Middle-Class Problem," *Class Unity* (January 03, 2022): https://classunity.org/2022/01/03/the-lefts-middle-class-problem-a-response-to-tempest/

Losurdo argues, "learning to build a bridge between the different temporalities" found in Marx's notion of communism – that is, on one end, the *utopian remote future* where "society inscribes on its banners: From each according to his ability, to each according to his needs!" and the *actual future* where communism is described as the "real movement which abolishes the present state of things."[10] Although this is important, I fear that a more profound change is required. Instead, I will conclude that a more accurate 'cure' is for Western Marxism to reflect on the objective conditions which drive its purity fetish, and once self-conscious of these, move towards both changing these objective conditions (which means moving away from a PMC dominated left and towards a working class centered left, free of the dominant influence of the PMC Iron Triangle institutions and culture), and towards stripping its purity fetish outlook – something which can only be done through the rearticulation of its ambiguous ideological elements towards a consistent dialectical materialist worldview.

---

[10] Losurdo, *Western Marxism,* 179; Marx and Engels, *MECW Vol. 24* (Moscow: Progress Publishers, 1989), 63; Marx and Engels, *MECW Vol. 5* (Moscow: Progress Publishers, 1976), 49.

I   The Philosophical Grounds of the Purity Fetish: Parmenides Contra Heraclitus, Hegel Contra Parmenides

The Western Marxist fixation on purity, staticity, homogeneity, etc. can be traced back to ancient Greek philosophy (500 or so years BC) and the debates which would take place over the question of change. Here, two central poles of thinking about change, the Eleatic and the Heraclitan, would arise.

The Eleatic school, headed by Parmenides and defended and developed by his most eminent disciples, Zeno and Melissus, held that "befuddled and helpless, as to resemble the deaf and blind," is the person who sustains that "to be and not to be are the same and not the same, and that everything is in a state of movement and counter-movement."[1] The two main principles of this school were "being is one" and "being is unchanging."[2] The 'one' here, however, was not understood as a heterogeneous one, a one which contains within itself the many – what Hegel and Marx would call the concrete. It was, instead, a homogenous one. To hold on to a dynamic many (to constantly interconnected plurality), was to participate in the way of opinion, and hence, to be devoid of truth. The appearance of contradiction, and the heterogeneity these imply in things and processes, were seen as impossible.

For instance, let us explore one (of four – according to Aristotle) of Zeno's paradoxes, where Eleatic thought reaches its most advanced form. As Aristotle notes, "the first asserts the nonexistence of motion on the ground that that which is in locomotion must arrive at the half-way stage before it arrives at the goal," and since there can be infinite divisibility, that is, infinite half-way stages, "it is," according to Zeno, "impossible for a thing to pass over or severally to come in contact with infinite things in a finite time."[3] For Zeno, this contradiction inherent in motion made the existence of motion impossible.

While Zeno is correct about the contradictory character of movement, "it does not follow," as Hegel would note, "that therefore there is no

---

[1] Phillip Wheelwright, *The Presocratics* (Indianapolis: The Odyssey Press, 1975), 97.
[2] Wheelwright, *The Presocratics*, 90.
[3] Aristotle, *Physics*. In *The Basic Works of Aristotle* (New York: Modern Library, 2001), 335 (239b), 320 (233a).

motion, but on the contrary, that motion is existent contradiction itself."[4] As the Polish Marxist Adam Schaff would later argue, "when investigating the possibility of movement Zeno *already* presumes that a body cannot 'be' or 'find itself' there otherwise than by *resting there*," his error, therefore, can be found in his "attempt to 'reduce' motion to a succession of states of rest."[5] When Zeno rightly arrives at the contradiction in the core of all change, instead of accepting that contradiction as the "root of all movement and vitality," he withdraws investigation and considers his discovery a sign of the falsehood of that which his discovery entails.[6]

In contradistinction to this school was Heraclitus, who developed a philosophy of universal flux, interconnection, and contradiction. For Heraclitus, "everything flows and nothing abides; everything gives way and nothing stays fixed."[7] In Heraclitus it is also held that "all things are one," but this 'one' is not homogeneous and static, it is a dynamic totality that is heterogeneous in character.[8] The many is contained within the one, neither the many nor the one, as in the Eleatics, is used to undermine the truth of the other. "In Heraclitus," as Hegel argues, "we see the perfection of the Idea into a totality, which is the beginning of philosophy, since it expresses the essence of the Idea, the Notion of the infinite, the potentially and actively existent, as that which it is, i.e., as the unity of opposites."[9] With Heraclitus "the dialectic itself [is] principle" and "the first concrete" category – becoming – arises and sublates the "abstract understanding" of the Eleatics' Being.[10] However, Heraclitus would lose – at least until the arrival of Hegel and Marxism – the worldview battle against Parmenides. Various aspects of Heraclitus' thought would become influential in scattered minds, but the anti-dialectical ethos of Eleatic philosophy would remain at the heart of Western thought for more than two millenniums. The Universal, truth, would continue to be thought in terms of the unchanging, of that

---

[4] G. W. F. Hegel, *Science of Logic*, Trans. A.V. Miller (Atlantic Highlands: Humanities Press International, 1993), 440.

[5] Adam Schaff, 'Marxist Dialectics and the Principle of Contradiction,' *The Journal of Philosophy* 57:7 (1960) 247, 248. https://doi.org/10.2307/2021865.

[6] Hegel, *Science of Logic*, 439. In this way, As Hegel would note in his *Lectures on the History of Philosophy*, "Kant's antinomies do no more than Zeno did." G. W. F. Hegel, *Lectures on the History of Philosophy Vol 1*(London: Routledge and Kegan Paul, 1974), 277.

[7] Wheelwright, *The Presocratics*, 70.

[8] Wheelwright, *The Presocratics*, 79.

[9] Hegel, *Lectures on the History of Philosophy Vol. 1*, 282.

[10] Hegel, *Lectures on the History of Philosophy Vol. 1*, 279, 283.

which is devoid of relationality and movement, in short, in terms of what Hegel calls the abstract understanding.

Plato, as the next best dialectician of the ancient world, attempted a reconciliation of Parmenides and Heraclitus. In the realm of Forms, the Parmenidean philosophy of permanence would reign; in the physical realm, the Heraclitan philosophy of flux would. In his *Phaedo*, for instance, Plato would note that the realm of the physical world is changing and composed of concrete opposites in an interpenetrative, i.e., dialectical, relationship to one another. In the realm of the "unchanging forms," however, "essential opposites will never… admit of generation into or out of one another."[11] Truth, ultimately, is in the realm of the Forms, where "purity, eternity, immortality, and unchangeableness" reign.[12] Hence, although attempting to provide a synthesis of Parmenides' and Heraclitus' philosophy of permanence and change, the philosophy of purity and fixation found in Parmenides dominates Plato's conception of the realm of the really real, that is, the realm of Forms or Idea. As Hegel puts it,

> This dialectic is, indeed, also a movement of thought, but it is really only necessary in an external way and for reflecting consciousness, in order to allow the universal, what is in and for itself, inalterable and immortal, to come forth. Hence [this dialectic], directed as [it is] towards the dissolution of the particular and thus to the production of the universal, [is] not yet dialectic in its true form: it is a dialectic which Plato has in common with the Sophists, who understood very well how to disintegrate the particular.[13]

The disintegration of the particular expressed a dialectic which was ontologically inferior to the Idea (realm of forms), where the dialectic was null, and where homogeneity, disconnection, and staticity reign. Plato's dialectic, however, is itself multiple, and appears in his large body of work in poorer and richer forms. For instance, the *Parmenides* is where Plato's most "genuine dialectic" is "fully worked-out."[14] Yet, the same distinction

---

[11] Plato, *Phaedo*. In *The Harvard Classics*. (New York: P.F. Collier & Son Corporation, 1937), 70, 90.
[12] Plato, *Phaedo*, 71.
[13] G. W. F. Hegel, *Lectures on the History of Philosophy Vol. 2* (London: Routledge and Kegan Paul, 1974), 52.
[14] Hegel, *Lectures on the History of Philosophy Vol. 2*, 56.

present in *Phaedo,* another one of his middle works, is found here. In his conversation with Zeno, Socrates says

> Tell me this: don't you acknowledge that there is a form, itself by itself, of likeness, and another form, opposite to this, which is what unlike is? Don't you and I and the other things we call 'many' get a share of those two entities? And don't things that get a share of likeness come to be like in that way and to the extent that they get a share, whereas things that get a share of unlikeness come to be unlike, and things that get a share of both come to be both? And even if all things get a share of both, though they are opposites, and by partaking of them are both like and unlike them-selves, what's astonishing about that? ... [But] if he could show that the kinds and forms themselves have in themselves these op-posite properties, that would call for astonishment.[15]

Again, the realm wherein truth does not delve allows for contradiction, movement, interconnection; the realm wherein truth does, that is, the realm of the essential Forms or Idea, does not. Additionally, even in the realm where dialectics embryonically exists, it is of a spurious character – it is a negative dialectic devoid of an affirmative reconciliation into something higher. In other words, it is a dialectic devoid of the negation of the nega-tion. As Hegel says, "the result arrived at in the *Parmenides* may not sat-isfy us, since it seems to be negative in character, and not, as the negation of the negation, expressive of true affirmation."[16]

Aristotle, a student of Plato, would move a step further away from the Heraclitan philosophy of flux. In Aristotle we have the development of the Western world's first logical system, an extremely impressive feat, but one composed of abstract and static categories, completely indifferent to con-tent and at odds with categorial interpenetration. For Aristotle, the most certain of all principles, of which there could be no demonstration for, is that "the same attribute cannot at the same time belong and not belong to the same subject and in the same respect."[17] This is what is known as the law of non-contradiction, out of which the law of identity (A is A) and the law of the excluded middle (A is either A or not-A) develop as well. The

---

[15] Plato, *Complete Works* (Indianapolis: Hackett Publishing Company, 1997), 362-363 (129a, 129b).
[16] Hegel, *Lectures on the History of Philosophy Vol. 2*, 60.
[17] Aristotle, *Metaphysics*. In *The Basic Works of Aristotle,* 736 (1005b15).

logic which organically follows from these laws of thought is the logic (i.e., science of thinking) for what Hegel calls the understanding, a form of thinking which foists disjunctions, staticity, and abstract generalities onto the world. As Hegel says of the three laws of thought (the heart of Aristotelean logic): these "are nothing but the law[s] of abstract under-standing."[18]

The fixation found in this logic would, of course, mirror the fixation and purity with which the *eidos* (essence) of things would be treated. Forms, although not existing in a separate realm as in Plato, nonetheless exist with the same rigidity. The thinking of essences, that is, the thinking of what makes a species, a type of thing, the type of thing it is, would remain in the realm of science within this fixated Aristotelian framework. Although the 16th century's scientific revolution begins to tear away the Aristotelianism which dominated the prevalent scholastic philosophy, only with the publication of Darwin's *On the Origin of Species* would Ar-istotelian essentialism be dealt a decisive blow. This essentialism, undeni-ably, is an inheritance of the Parmenidean philosophy of permanence. These limitations in dialectical thought, however, do not take away from the fact that Aristotle was, as Hegel says, "one of the richest and deepest of all the scientific geniuses that have as yet appeared – a man who's like no later age has ever produced."[19]

The philosophy of Plato, in the form of Neo-Platonists like Plotinus and others, would be incredibly influential in the formation of Christian thought – especially in Augustine of Hippo. Therefore, when dialectics showed up, it was in the poorer forms found in Plato's dialectic. If we recall the critique of the negative dialectic in Plato's *Parmenides* we es-poused above, "the Neo-Platonists, [like the late Neo-Platonist Proclus]," Hegel would argue, "regard the result arrived at in the *Parmenides* as the true theology, as the revelation of all the mysteries of the divine essence."[20] Christianity would remain with a Platonic philosophical foundation up un-til the 12th-13th century's rediscovery of Aristotle and the synthetization of his philosophy with Christian doctrine *via* Thomas Aquinas. Centuries later the protestant reformation's rejection of Aristotelianism would mark the return of Plato to the Christian scene.

---

[18] G. W. F. Hegel, *Hegel's Logic: Being Part One of the Encyclopaedia of the Philosophical Sci-ences*, Translated by W. Wallace (Oxford: Clarendon Press, 1874), 184.
[19] Hegel, *Lectures on the History of Philosophy Vol. 2*, 117. Marx and Engels would argue that He-gel was for the modern world what Aristotle was for the ancient.
[20] Hegel, *Lectures on the History of Philosophy Vol. 2*, 60.

All in all, the Christian messianism which Manoel and Losurdo see as the root of the fetishization of purity in every moment of its unfolding presupposes a very particular line of Greek philosophy. It is fair, then, to go beyond Christianity and ask the critical question: what is presupposed here? What we find is that in every instance, whether mediated through Plato or Aristotle, there is a Parmenidean worldview which posits the homogeneous one, eternal and unchanging as synonymous with truth, and the dynamic, heterogeneous, and many as synonymous with false.

Nonetheless, what Hegel says with regards to Plato can be said with regards to the Parmenidean worldview's dominance in the history of Western philosophy:

> Plato's point of view is clearly defined and necessary, but it is impossible for us to remain there, or to go back to it; for Reason now makes higher demands ... We must stand above Plato, i.e., we must acquaint ourselves with the needs of thoughtful minds in our own time, or rather we must ourselves experience these needs ... [Platonic philosophy is a] moment which [has its] due place and [its] own importance, but [it is] not the philosophy of our time.[21]

The Eleatic purity fetish worldview has been a necessary moment in the development of what Hegel would call world spirit (weltgeist), or what in the Marxist tradition we may call (with Ilyenkov) the Ideal. The "reproduction of the concrete by way of thought," as Marx notes (along with Hegel), is "not a point of departure" but the result of "a process of concentration."[22] Abstract thought, as I have argued before, is "a necessary moment in [the] ascension towards the concrete reproduction of the concrete."[23] However, as necessary a moment (or moments) this dominance of the Eleatic abstract and static worldview was, it was bound to be historically sublated by the return of the Heraclitan worldview, but in the more concrete and advanced forms in which it appears in the philosophy of

---

[21] Hegel, *Lectures on the History of Philosophy Vol. 2*, 10.

[22] Karl Marx, *Grundrisse* (London: Penguin Books, 1973), 100.

[23] Carlos L. Garrido, "The Dialectical Ascension from the Abstract to the Concrete," *Midwestern Marx Institute for Marxist Theory and Political Analysis* (July 28, 2022: https://www.midwestern-marx.com/articles/the-dialectical-ascension-from-the-abstract-to-the-concrete-by-carlos-l-garrido; Carlos L. Garrido, *Marxism and the Dialectical Materialist Worldview: An Anthology of Classical Marxist Texts on Dialectical Materialism* (Midwestern Marx Publishing Press, 2022), 35.

Hegel and, in an even more concrete form, in the Marxist dialectical materialist worldview. While Heraclitus's dialectical worldview suffered many lost battles over two millenniums, it would come back with Hegel and Marxism equipped to win the war. As Hegel rightly argues,

> If truth is abstract it must be untrue … [for] what is true is rather found in motion, in a process … the true is concrete, [and] must occur in the onward course of philosophical development. Philosophy is what is most antagonistic to abstraction, and it leads back to the concrete …it is the business of philosophy, as opposed to understanding, to show that the Truth or the Idea does not consist in empty generalities, but in a universal; and that is within itself the particular and the determined. It is just this unity of differences which is the concrete… [the concrete] is the union of the different determinations.[24]

The spirit of the Heraclitan dialectic will be rekindled by G. W. F. Hegel, who would argue that philosophy came to finally see "land" with Heraclitus.[25] In his *Lectures on the History of Philosophy*, Hegel says that "there is no proposition of Heraclitus which I have not adopted in my Logic."[26] It is in Heraclitus, Hegel argues, where we "see the perfection of knowledge so far as it has gone;" for, Heraclitus "understands the absolute as just this process of the dialectic."[27] Heraclitus' dialectics understood, as Hegel notes, that "being and non-being are abstractions devoid of truth, that the first truth is to be found in becoming."[28] This unity of pure being and nothing is the starting point for Hegel's *Science of Logic*. Here, he argues:

> [Pure] being, the indeterminate immediate, is in fact nothing, and neither more nor less than nothing… Pure being and nothing are, therefore, the same. What is truth is neither being nor nothing, but that being – does not pass over but has passed over – into nothing, and nothing into being.[29]

---

[24] Hegel, *Lectures on the History of Philosophy Vol. 1*, 24, 25; Hegel, *Lectures on the History of Philosophy Vol. 2*, 13.
[25] Hegel, *Lectures on the History of Philosophy Vol. 1*, 279.
[26] Hegel, *Lectures on the History of Philosophy Vol. 1*, 279.
[27] Hegel, *Lectures on the History of Philosophy Vol. 1*, 278.
[28] Hegel, *Lectures on the History of Philosophy Vol. 1*, 283.
[29] Hegel, *Science of Logic*, 82-83.

Insofar as being exists in a condition of purity, it is indistinguishable from nothingness. Being must take the risk of facing and tarrying with its opposite in order to *be*. Being only takes place within the impurity present in the oscillation from being and nothing, that is, being only takes place when sublated into becoming *qua* determinate being, as "coming-to-be and ceasing-to-be."[30] In fact, what Hegel shows is that, all along, this idea of 'pure being' was not so pure – that is, when thoroughly examined, it already contained within itself an identity with its opposite – nothing. An essential point is made in this first movement in Hegel's *Logic*, namely, the determinateness of all categories is a result of tarrying with its negative. As Hegel scholar Terry Pinkard argues, "the logic of other more developed conceptions of being are constructed according to the logic of the conception of pure being: each conception of being takes its determinateness, as it were, from its own 'nothing,' from what Hegel calls its *negation*."[31] As Ian Hunt and Roy Swan concisely put it, "the whole method is implicit … in the first triad of Being."[32] The seeming (Schein) desecration of a category when confronted with its other is always the condition for the possibility of escaping empty immediacy, of becoming determinate as mediated immediacy, as a positive which has been mediated – and hence, is conscious of it containing within itself – the negative.

This is why, in his *Phenomenology of Spirit*, Hegel says that "Substance is being which is in truth Subject."[33] Substance (in Greek *ousia* and Latin *substantia*), whose foundational purity holds the crowning jewel of Truth for Western philosophy, can be only insofar as it is "self-othering" itself.[34] Far from being in a unilateral relationship of necessity with subject, with subject existing *qua* determined by substance, this relation is reciprocal – substance can only be as substance in so far as it is through subject. In substance as in subject, the negative is contained as an indispensable component of the conceptual identity of each. Substance must, as Hegel argues, look the "negative in the face, and tarry with it."[35] When it does this, it finds that its conceptual identity contains, "not externally,

---

[30] Hegel, *Science of Logic*, 103.
[31] Terry Pinkard, *Hegel's Dialectic* (Philadelphia: Temple University Press, 1988), 26.
[32] Ian Hunt and Roy Swan, "A Comparison of Marxist and Hegelian Dialectical Form," *Radical Philosophy*, Vol. 30 (Spring 1982) 33-40, 35.
[33] G. W. F. Hegel, *Phenomenology of Spirit* (Oxford: Oxford University Press, 1977), 10.
[34] Hegel, *Phenomenology of Spirit*, 10.
[35] Hegel, *Phenomenology of Spirit*, 19.

but in its own self, in its very nature," difference (i.e., impurity, the negative).[36] Only insofar as something can self-otherize itself, which is to say, only insofar as a thing can immanently provide a negation for itself and desecrate its purity by wrestling with the impure, can conditions for the possibility of it being *actual* arise. Hence, the "truth of being" is "characterized as Becoming;" truth is won "only when, in utter dismemberment, it finds itself."[37] This is true regardless of the different forms of mediation that negation takes in the logic of being (transition), the logic of essence (reflection), and the logic of notion (development).

Purity, the "[shrinking] from death [to] keep untouched by devastation," is lifeless.[38] Jay cannot be with Daisy insofar as he wishes to retain the relationship in purity. Western Marxists will never build socialism, or find a socialism to support, insofar as they expect socialism or the working class to arise in the pure forms in which it exists in their heads.

Now that the philosophical ground of Western Marxism's purity fetish has been developed and shown to be rooted in a very particular line of Greek philosophy (and only indirectly in Christian mysticism), let us turn to the variety of ways this outlook manifests itself in Western Marxism.

---

[36] Hegel, *Science of Logic*, 413.
[37] Hegel, *Lectures on the History of Philosophy Vol.1*, 283; *Phenomenology of Spirit*, 19.
[38] Hegel, *Phenomenology of Spirit*, 19.

II - The Paradoxes of Western Marxism

Having shifted our focus from Christianity to the purity fetish worldview of Western philosophy, we can now see one of the fundamental paradoxes in Western Marxism: on the one hand, in hopes of differentiating themselves from the 'positivistic' and 'mechanistic' Marxism that arose in the Soviet Union, it claims to return to Hegel (or to a more Hegelianized young Marx) in their fight against 'orthodox dogma;' on the other hand, although it has the capability of producing laudable works on Hegel and dialectics, Western Marxism's interpretive lens for looking at the world remains within a Parmenidean rigidity and Aristotelian form of binary thinking.[1] Western Marxists, although claiming to be the ones who rekindle the spirit of Hegel into Marxism, are, ironically, the least dialectical when it comes to analysis of the concrete world. We can say of Western Marxists something akin to what Lenin said of Kautsky, Bauer and others of the second international:

> they themselves learned Marxist dialectic and taught it to others (and much of what they have done in this field will always remain a valuable contribution to socialist literature); however, in the application of this dialectic they… proved to be so undialectical in practice, so incapable of taking into account the rapid change of forms and the rapid acquisition of new content by the old forms, that their fate is not much more enviable than that of Hyndman, Guesde and Plekhanov.[2]

They are unable to understand, as Hegel did, the necessary role apparent 'failures' play as a moment in the unfolding of truth. For Hegel, that which is seen as 'false' is part of "the process of distinguishing in general" and constitutes an "essential moment" of Truth.[3] The bud (one of Hegel's favorite examples which consistently reappears in his work) is not proven

---

[1] For instance, works like Marcuse's *Reason and Revolution;* Adorno's *Hegel: Three Studies;* Anderson's *Lenin, Hegel and Western Marxism,* are commendable texts of Hegel – or Hegel adjacent – scholarship.

[2] V. I. Lenin, *Collected Works Vol. 31* (New York: International Publishers, 1974), 102.

[3] Hegel, *Phenomenology of Spirit,* 23.

'false' when the blossom arises. Instead, Hegel notes, each sustains a "mutual necessity" as "moments of an organic unity."[4]

Socialism is not 'betrayed' when it, encountering the external and internal pressures of imperialism and a national bourgeois class, is forced to take more so-called 'authoritarian' positions to protect the revolution. Socialism is not 'betrayed' or transformed into 'state capitalism' (in the derogatory, non-Leninist sense) when faced with a backwards economy it takes the risk of tarrying with its opposite and engages a process of opening up to foreign capital to develop its productive forces.

The 'authoritarian' moment, or the moment of 'opening up to foreign capital,' are not an annihilating negation of socialism – as Western Marxists would have you believe – but the sublation of the idealistic conceptions of a 'pure' socialism, especially in its earliest stages. These two moments instead present themselves as the historically necessary negations needed to develop socialism. A socialist Russia that had not taken the 'strategic retreat' towards Lenin's New Economic Policy amidst the onslaught of the difficulties of 'war communism' (which were forced upon them following their invasion by fifteen countries, including the UK, the US, Japan, Italy, et. al.) would not have survived. Likewise, without the so-called 'Stalinist' collectivization, not only would the Soviet Union have remained unindustrialized and poor, but the Hitlerite forces would have been able to – as the West expected (and hoped) – trample over the 'Judeo-Bolshevik' menace, destroying the first worker state and the notion that working class people could, indeed, rule themselves .[5]

Similarly, a less 'authoritarian' treatment of the Batista goons after the Cuban revolution would have opened the window for imperialism and national counter-revolutionary forces to overthrow the popular revolution. A less 'authoritarian' Democratic People's Republic of Korea (DPRK) would not have survived the hybrid warfare waged on it by the US empire (and its NATO lackeys), who killed twenty percent of their population during the war and who have strangled their country with one of the most aggressive sanction regimes in the world for 70 years straight. The 'authoritarianism' that the Western Marxist's purity fetish condemns is in every instance a necessary component to protect a revolution's sovereignty and socialist democracy. But, since they treat 'authoritarianism'

---

[4] Hegel, *Phenomenology of Spirit*, 2.
[5] For more see Domenico Losurdo, *Stalin: The History and Critique of a Black Legend*, translated by David Ferreira (Open Source, 2020).

and 'democracy' abstractly; failing to ask: 'democracy for which class?' and 'authoritarianism against which class?' – they are unable to see the necessary role 'authoritarianism' against imperialism, and against the national classes which collaborate with imperialism, plays in securing a richer, broader, and more developed form of socialist democracy for the common people.

Likewise, a China which would not have taken the frightening risk of 'opening up' in 1978 would not have been able to lift 800 million people out of poverty (eradicating extreme poverty in the country) and be the beacon of socialist construction and anti-imperialist resistance in the world today. As Samir Amin eloquently states with regards to China,

> China bashing panders to the infantile opinion found in some currents of the powerless Western left: if it is not the communism of the twenty-third century, it is a betrayal![6]

The Western Marxist purity fetish fails to see that *purity is itself impossible*; that all things, whether in nature, society, or thought, are heterogeneous and complex entities, necessarily in process and interconnected to all things within a totality that it both shapes and is emergently shaped by. As Lenin argued in 'The Collapse of the Second International,'

> There are *no* "pure" phenomena, nor can there be, either in Nature or in society—that is what Marxist dialectics teaches us, for dialectics shows that the very concept of purity indicates a certain narrowness, a one-sidedness of human cognition, which cannot embrace an object in all its totality and complexity.[7]

Hegel understood that every leap towards a qualitatively new stage required a long process, consisting of various moments of 'failures' and 'successes,' for this new stage to mature into its new shape. Using for Spirit the metaphor of a child he says,

> But just as the first breath drawn by a child after its long, quiet nourishment breaks the gradualness of merely quantitative growth-

---

[6] Samir Amin, *Only People Make Their Own History: Writings on Capitalism, Imperialism, and Revolution* (New York: Monthly Review Press, 2019), 110.
[7] V. I. Lenin, *Collected Works Vol. 21* (New York: International Publishers, 1974) 236.

there is a qualitative leap, and the child is born-so likewise the Spirit in its formation matures slowly and quietly into its new shape, dissolving bit by bit the structure of its previous world, whose tottering state is only hinted at by isolated symptoms.[8]

Western Marxists ignore the necessity of process. They expect socialism, a qualitatively new stage of human history, to exist immediately in the pure form they conceived of in their minds. They expect a child to act like a grown up and find themselves angered when the child is unable to recite Shakespeare and solve algebraic equations. They fail to see that those things they condemn in socialist states are not only forced upon them, but also not eternal. Instead of seeing these, as Evald Ilyenkov would argue, "as signs of the movement's historical immaturity," they essentialize and eternalize what is of historical (i.e., contextual) necessity.[9] They forget, therefore, to contextualize whatever deficiencies they might observe within the embryonic stage the global movement towards socialism is in. They forget the world is still dominated by capitalist imperialism and expect the pockets of socialist resistance to be purely cleansed from the corrupting influence of the old world. They forget that these conditions necessarily lead the early stages of socialist construction to be, as Michael Parenti notes, a *siege socialism*, constantly having to fight against what Vijay Prashad calls *hybrid warfare* from the global imperialist forces.[10] They forget, as Marx noted in his *Critique of the Gotha Program*, that socialist society exists "as it emerges from capitalist society which is thus in every respect, economically, morally and intellectually, still stamped with the birth marks of the old society from whose womb it emerges."[11]

---

[8] Hegel, *Phenomenology of Spirit*, 6.

[9] Evald Ilyenkov, "From the Marxist-Leninist Point of View." In *Marx and the Western World*, ed. Nicholas Lobkowicz (London: University of Notre Dame Press, 1967), 403.

[10] Michael Parenti, *Black Shirts and Reds: Rational Fascism and the Overthrow of Communism* (San Francisco: City Lights Books, 1997), 49. Vijay Prashad, *Washington Bullets* (Neh Dehli: Leftword Books, 2020), 133-134. "To have 'full-spectrum dominance' over a society requires more than that – it requires a hybrid war that includes sabotage and economic blockades as well as cultural and media campaigns to undermine the truth. The hybrid war is a combination of unconventional and conventional means using a range of state and non-state actors that run across the spectrum of social and political life. Part of this hybrid warfare is the battle over ideas, with the United States and its oligarchic allies smothering hostile countries by sabotage and economic blockades and then egging on the population to act in a 'colour revolution' against the government. Once the regime is changed, there is no political weight for the people themselves to craft a new government which is more attuned to popular hopes."

[11] Marx and Engels, *MECW Vol. 24, 63*.

The Only Acceptable Impurity is Imperialism: Controlled Counter-Hegemony and the Compatible Left

One of the paradoxes in Western Marxism's purity fetish can be seen in the fact that the imperialist West is hardly ever too 'impure' to support in its battles against the red menace. Adorno and Horkheimer, for instance, frequently showed "support for the U.S.'s anti-communist puppet government in West Germany, whose intelligence services had been stocked with former Nazis;" the same Nazis the pair repeatedly compared the Soviet Union with while peddling distinctly Hitlerite ideas which argued that: "the threat that the East will engulf the foothills of Western Europe is obvious," as Adorno stated, "and whoever fails to resist it is literally guilty of repeating Chamberlain's *appeasement.*"[12] This same duo, today promoted as Marxism *par excellence* in the academy, supported the US's barbaric invasion of Vietnam with the sort of rhetoric commonly heard from the most far-right elements of US politics. As Horkheimer stated in 1967, "in America, when it is necessary to conduct a war… it is not so much a question of the defense of the homeland, but it is essentially a matter of the defense of the constitution, the defense of the rights of man."[13]

As the Cold War developed, the Congress for Cultural Freedom (CCF), a "secret programme of cultural propaganda in Western Europe," was one of the most important developments in imperialism's global fight against communism.[14] "At its peak," Frances Stoner Saunders writes,

> The Congress for Cultural Freedom had offices in thirty-five countries, employed dozens of personnel, published over twenty prestige magazines, held art exhibitions, owned a news and features service, organized high-profile international conferences, and rewarded musicians and artists with prizes and public performances.[15]

---

[12] Rockhill, "The CIA and the Frankfurt School's Anti-Communism,;" Theodor Adorno, *Critical Models: Interventions and Catchwords*, trans. Henry W. Pickford (New York: Columbia University Press, 2005), 94.

[13] Wolfgang Kraushaar, ed., *Frankfurter Schule und Studentenbewegung: Von der Flaschenpost zum Molotowcocktail 1946-1995*, Vol. I: *Chronik* (Hamburg: Rogner & Bernhard GmbH & Co. Verlags KG, 1998), 252-3. Quoted from Rockhill, "The CIA and the Frankfurt School's Anti-Communism."

[14] Frances Stoner Saunders, *The Cultural Cold War: The CIA and the World of Arts and Letters* (New York: The New Press, 1990), 1.

[15] Saunders, *The Cultural Cold War*, 1.

"Its mission" was the following: "to nudge the intelligentsia of western Europe away from its lingering fascination with Marxism and Communism towards a view more accommodating of 'the American way.'"[16] Both Adorno and Horkheimer participated in CCF related projects. Adorno, for instance, "published in the CIA-funded journal *Der Monat*," "in two other CIA magazines: *Encounter* and *Tempo presente*," and "corresponded and collaborated with the CIA operative who was arguably the leading figure in the German anticommunist *Kulturkampf*: Melvin Lasky."[17]

"As critical as they sometimes are of capitalism," Adorno and Horkheimer "regularly affirm that there is no alternative."[18] Naturally, when abstract terms like 'totalitarianism' or 'authoritarianism' are used to equalize communism and fascism on the basis of unsubstantiated anti-communist stories out of the imperialist West, liberal democracy shines forth as the 'best of all possible worlds.' In the decades after the Soviets lost 27 million souls saving the world from Fascism, here were these 'Marxists' claiming that the communists were as bad as the fascists, often "invoking racist descriptions of the 'barbarians' in the East, whom they describe using the overtly sub-humanizing vocabulary of 'beasts' and 'hordes' they flatly proclaim ... are 'fascists' who have chosen 'slavery.'"[19] Adorno and Horkheimer's anti-communism – a general feature of Western Marxism's purity fetish – highlights the foresight of Marshal Zhukov's famous dictum, 'The Soviet Union liberated Europe from fascism, but they will never forgive us for it.' The service the Soviet Union did for humanity would not be appreciated by many of those in the West, who like Adorno and Horkheimer, denounced the USSR while simultaneously claiming to be rooted in the same tradition – i.e., Marxism. The paradox here is that, on the subject of the Soviet system, the CIA was itself to the 'left' of these 'Marxists.' As a 1955 CIA document, accessible thanks to the Freedom of Information Act, says

> Even in Stalin's time there was collective leadership. The Western idea of a dictator within the Communist setup is exaggerated.

---

[16] Saunders, *The Cultural Cold War*, 1.
[17] Rockhill, "The CIA and the Frankfurt School's Anti-Communism."
[18] Rockhill, "The CIA and the Frankfurt School's Anti-Communism."
[19] Rockhill, "The CIA and the Frankfurt School's Anti-Communism."

> Misunderstandings on that subject are caused by lack of comprehension of the real nature and organization of the Communist power structure. Stalin, although holding wide powers, was merely the captain of a team.[20]

While Herbert Marcuse was a half-step up from Adorno and Horkheimer's condemnations of communism and anti-colonial movements in the global south and Middle East, he was still working within an outlook deeply embedded in the purity fetish. At the height of the Vietnam War, Marcuse correctly asserted that "Vietnam is not just another affair in international politics, but rather a fact intimately linked to the very essence of the system."[21] Additionally, he was able to connect the US' invasion of Vietnam to its treatment of its black population at home and argued for the need to connect anti-colonial struggles (such as Vietnam's) to the struggles within the metropole.[22] Nonetheless, although supportive of the Vietnamese people's struggles, he would still argue that their fight – led by Ho Chi Minh and the Communist Party of Vietnam – had "nothing to do with building a socialist society."[23] Because it failed to live up to his 'pure' idea of what socialism ought to be like, what they were constructing was *not actually socialism*.

A similar half-step up is seen in his treatment of the Soviet Union. While he recognizes the difficulties presented for the construction of socialism in backward conditions and under constant imperialist attacks, he nonetheless condemns this socialist construction as totalitarian and qualitatively indistinguishable from the capitalist mode of life. Marcuse understood that in this context, the Soviet Union was necessarily on the defensive, and needed to focus first on the centralized development of the forces of production, science, and technologies. The Soviets needed, as Lenin noted shortly after the conquest of power, to develop an efficient state that could protect the revolution and country's sovereignty and lift the people's standards of living in the process. Forced to choose between "capitulating to colonialism and imperialism, or accelerating economic and technological development," Marcuse argues the Soviet Union needed "power of

---

[20] Central Intelligence Agency, "Comments on the Change in Soviet Leadership," *Freedom of Information Act*: https://www.cia.gov/readingroom/document/cia-rdp80-00810a006000360009-0
[21] Herbert Marcuse, *La fine dell'utopia*, trans. by S. Vertone, (Laterza, Bari, 1968). Quoted in Losurdo, *Western Marxism*, 88.
[22] Marcuse, *La fine dell'utopia*; Losurdo, *Western Marxism*, 88-89.
[23] Marcuse, *La fine dell'utopia*, 57, 65, 73; Losurdo, *Western Marxism*, 90.

total administration [so that] automation [could] proceed more rapidly once a certain technical level has been attained."[21] Only in doing so would it successfully defend itself from the imperialist challenge.

Nonetheless, while recognizing this, Marcuse still condemned Soviet 'totalitarianism' in similar unsubstantiated ways as can be found in Adorno and Horkheimer. However, unlike Adorno and Horkheimer, Marcuse's condemnation is far more infantile, for he recognizes how the Soviet Union is put on the defensive and limited by Western imperialism, yet he condemns them for doing precisely what he himself understands they were forced to do. The purity fetish here couldn't be any more apparent: because the Soviet Union failed to live up to Marcuse's 'pure' socialism, it is condemned and held to be no different – in substance – from the capitalist mode of life. It is thanks to the purity fetish and his "inability to carry dialectical thinking onto his analysis of the socialist camp" that Marcuse is able to posit the thesis of a global "one-dimensional reality."[25] The socialist 'camp,' because it was forced to desecrate its purity to protect its revolution, was now – for Marcuse – insufficiently different from the capitalist-imperialist world, and hence, not an alternative to the global system, but one component, or a form, of it. This is hardly different, for instance, from Horkheimer's condemnation of the USSR as "state capitalism" (again, in the derogatory, non-Leninist sense).[26] In both cases it is argued that the socialism of the USSR is not qualitatively different from the global capitalist system – if anything, it is just a more 'authoritarian' and 'statist' form of it.

While Marcuse's *One-Dimensional Man* critiques the anti-dialectical character of those who pass judgments based only on reified "facts and not the factors" which led those facts into existence, he himself performs this anti-dialectical castration of facts in his equalization of the socialist and capitalist camp as interdependent systems of a global "one-dimensional civilization."[27] For Marcuse to say that the socialist camp, like capitalism, "exploits the productivity of labor and capital without structural resistance, while considerably reducing working hours and augmenting the comforts

---

[24] Domenico Losurdo, *Western Marxism*, 90. Herbert Marcuse, *One-Dimensional Man* (New York: Routledge, 2007), 41.
[25] Carlos L. Garrido, "The Relevance and Failures of Marcuse's One-Dimensional Man," *Hampton Institute* (May 31, 2021): https://www.hamptonthink.org/read/the-relevance-and-failures-of-marcuses-one-dimensional-man ; Marcuse, *One-Dimensional Man*, 128.
[26] Max Horkheimer, "Lo Stato authoritario," in *La società de transizione*, ed. by W. Bre de (Einaudi, Turin, 1979), 4.
[27] Marcuse, *One-Dimensional Man*, 187, 66.

of life," he must ignore the conditions, both present and historical, that allowed this fact to arise.[28]

Capitalism was able to achieve this 'comfortable' life for its working masses because it spent the last three centuries colonizing the world to ensure that the resources of foreign lands would be disposable to Western capital. This course of Western capitalist enrichment required a brutal process of enclosure and colonization (the so-called 'primitive accumulation'), creating mass pauperization (in Europe) and conquests of foreign lands wherein aboriginal peoples faced genocidal treatment and Africans enslavement. Then, in the last decade of the 19th century, when the development of capitalism reached the stage of modern imperialism, this carnage was extended in much broader dimensions, producing two World Wars, Nazism, and further massacres and genocides of colonized peoples. Capitalism, as Marx said, "comes dripping from head to foot, from every pore, with blood and dirt."[29]

The overwhelming majority of the fruits from this on-going process of expropriation and exploitation, however, are not going to the working classes of the Western nations, and the very small portion of it that does, is not because of the generosity of the capitalist class. It is true, as Lenin said (with Engels), that "a privileged upper stratum of the proletariat in the imperialist countries lives partly at the expense of hundreds of millions in the uncivilised nations."[30] It is true that the right opportunist and social chauvinist segments of the "upper stratum" of the labor movement have been "bribed out of imperialist superprofits."[31] But the key here is to note that Lenin is speaking of "the petty bourgeoisie and of a certain [upper] strata of the working class;" he is not referring to the whole working class of imperialist countries.[32] The few 'comforts' Marcuse can point to have been the result of century-long labor struggles in the US (or Europe), most frequently led by communists, socialists, and militant labor unions. Capitalism has provided no comforts for working people; it has been the organized working class which, through its struggles, has forced concessions from the capitalist class and its political puppets – concessions strategically given to prevent more radical transformations.

---

[28] Marcuse, *One-Dimensional Man*, 46.

[29] Karl Marx, *Capital Vol. I* (New York: International Publishers, 1974) 760.

[30] V. I. Lenin, *Collected Works Vol. 23* (Moscow: Progress Publishers, 1974), 107

[31] Lenin, *CW Vol. 23*, 107.

[32] Lenin, *CW Vol. 23*, 110.

For Marcuse, since the working class of the imperialist countries has been fully absorbed into the existing state of affairs, it is no longer a revolutionary class. This, naturally, leads to either 1) the miserable pessimism of texts like *One-Dimensional Man*, or 2) the idea that all the work must be done by the third world. In either case, his positions do not threaten the capitalist class of the imperialist core – if workers are told by the Marxists that they can't change capitalism because they benefit from it, then they won't fight for socialism: the ruling class, therefore, is spared. Similarly, if because of this condition, workers are told that they must wait for the third world to free itself before they can be free, then the third world is given all the weight of the global struggle for socialism – while the 'exceptional' Western Marxists get to just sit around with their hands in their pockets waiting for the global south to do all the work. This position is not only detrimental to the working class struggle in the imperialist core, but also for the struggles of the periphery, which would be infinitely easier if the boot of imperialist hybrid warfare were removed from their necks by socialist revolution in the imperialist core. As ever-brilliant Henry Winston notes,

> In Marcuse's view, the working class was hopelessly reactionary and contentedly integrated into the system – the upholders, not the gravediggers, of capitalism … [This] style of attacks on Marxism-Leninism in the name of 'revolution' changes, it sometimes seems, almost as frequently as traffic lights. And these 'revolutionary' assaults – which always have as their core a challenge to the Marxist-Leninist concept of the leading role of the industrial working class – receive more than a mere passive welcome from monopoly. Monopoly subsidizes, promotes, and publicizes them through its centers of education and mass media.[33]

Similar variations of this position are often found in the ultra-left segments of the US left – specifically in certain communist and anarchist spaces.[34]

---

[33] Henry Winston, *Class, Race and Black Liberation* (New York: International Publishers, 1977), 215.

[34] The book *Settlers: The Myth of the White Proletariat*, written by the state department connected anonymous anarchist J Sakai, has been making the rounds on the communist left over the last few years. It has resurfaced at a time when the fad in radical academia and certain communist groups has been referring to the US today as a 'settler-colonial' project. The ideological leader in this regard has indubitably been Gerald Horne and his book *The Counter-Revolution of 1776*, which – in hopes of historically tracing the reactions to Obama and the roots of the Trump movement – posits that the

The difference is the following: instead of considering the working class as workers which have been absorbed by the niceties of the imperial core (Marcuse's position), the working class – or at least the 70 percent of it which is white – are considered to be 'settlers,' not workers. These settlers are necessary foot soldiers of the settler-colonial American project. Far from being a revolutionary class in an antagonistic relationship to capital, this relatively new ultra-leftism holds that the white proletariat is a *myth*; in reality, what exists is a 'settler' class. Although these views are far more extreme than Marcuse's, both end up in a deeply pessimistic position concerning the revolutionary potential of the working class in the imperialist core; and, in so far as the practical implications align with the goals of the capitalist class, both have been safely adopted by radical bourgeois media, academia, and NGO's.

Marcuse's anti-dialectical equalization of the socialist and capitalist camp also ignores the fact that the socialist camp industrialized their backwards countries in a fraction of the time it took the West, without having to colonize lands, genocide natives, or enslave blacks – the heinous crimes which are the background of capitalism's development. On the contrary, the industrialization process in the socialist camp was (and is – e.g., China's Belt and Road Initiative) inextricably linked to the empowering of the peripheral subjects, whether African, Asian, Middle Eastern, or Indo-American, that had been under the boot of western colonialism and imperialism for centuries. The 'third-world' that Marcuse assigns the role of historical subjectivity (in texts like *One-Dimensional Man* and others), was in large part able to sustain autonomy because of the solidarity and aid – political, military, or economic, that it received from the socialist camp. Those who were unable to establish relations with the socialist camp (for whatever reason), often replicated – in a neo-colonial fashion – the relations they had with their metropoles. The central difference was that

---

American revolution was actually a counter-revolution to protect the institute of slavery. This 'settler colonialism' framework dismisses all previous Marxist understandings of the US Revolutionary war (more on this in the last chapter of this book) and, in so doing, provides a framework for understanding the development of US society which is completely contrary to the Marxist dialectical materialist worldview. Unable to tarry with objective contradictions, development and process, qualitative leaps which occur as a result of quantitative accumulation, and other basic dialectical laws of movement observable in nature, society, and thought, this framework ends up, like Marcuse, in a deeply pessimistic position concerning the revolutionary potential of the working class in the imperialist core. This is why, similar to Marcuse, its 'radicalism' is enjoyed and disseminated in the halls of bourgeois media, NGOs, and academia. The *1619 Project*, explicitly inspired by Horne's book, is a good example of this.

the dominance of the European nation was no longer explicit – it was carried out under the veil of superficial Western-style bourgeois democracies (in the former colonies) which were controlled through debt-trapping by Euro-American dominated global financial institutions like the International Monetary Fund and the World Bank. Through structural adjustment programs, the Western imperialist powers could ensure that an agenda of liberalization, austerity, privatization, and deregulation were carried out in the neo-colonies, making them fertile for Western monopoly capital to continue and expand its looting and superexploitation of these nations. These processes were broadened and intensified after the overthrow of the socialist camp, which left the countries in the third world which sustained an autonomous position (thanks to the comradely relations they established with the socialist world), to be quickly re-subjected to serve Western capital (with the exceptions of Cuba and the DPRK).

By stating that the socialist camp was unable to affect a materialization of its theory in practice, and as such, that it was not qualitatively different from capitalism (making the equating of the two possible), Marcuse effectively demonstrates his ignorance, willful or not, of both the geopolitical situation of the time and of the theory itself. Socialism in the 20th century could not create its ideal qualitatively new society while simultaneously defending its revolution from imperialist hybrid warfare coming from the largest imperial powers in the history of humanity. It is idealist and infantile to expect the struggle for socialism to resemble the 'pure' socialist ideal in a world where the dominant form of global relations is capitalist.

Nonetheless, even Marcuse is forced to admit that the socialist camp was able to create a comfortable life for its working masses. But, contrary to what Marcuse argues, this comfort in the socialist camp cannot be equated with comfort in the capitalist camp. Not only are the conditions that led to the comfort in each fundamentally different (as just previously examined), but the comfort itself, as a *fact*, was also radically different. In terms of job security, housing, healthcare, education, childcare, and other forms of government provided social securities, the comfort in the socialist camp was significantly higher than the comfort experienced by the working masses in the welfare social democracies of Europe, and tenfold that of the comfort experienced by the working masses in the US. When you add to this the ability for political participation through worker councils and the party, the prevalent spirit of solidarity that reigned, and the general absence of racism and crime, the foolishness of the equalization is further highlighted. Nonetheless, the comparison must not only be made between the capitalist and socialist camp, but between the conditions before and after the socialist camp achieved socialism. Only in doing so can we historically contextualize the achievements of the socialist camp in terms of creating dignified and freer lives for hundreds of millions of people. For these people, Marcuse's comments are somewhere between laughable and symbolic of the usual disrespect and social chauvinism found in the purity fetish of Western Marxism.

Although Marcuse was unable to live long enough to see it, the fall of the socialist camp, and the subsequent 'shock therapy' that went with it, not only devastated the countries of the previous socialist camp – drastically raising the rates of poverty, crime, prostitution, and inequality, while lowering the standard of living, life expectancy, and opportunities for political participation – but also the countries of the third world and those of the capitalist camp themselves![35] With the threat of communism seemingly gone, the mass resources of the third-world (and those of the post-Soviet states) were up for grabs again, and the first world, no longer under the pressure of the alternative that a comfortable working mass in the socialist camp presented, was free to extend the wrath of capital back into its own national popular classes, eroding century long victories in the labor movement and creating the conditions for precarious, unregulated, and more exploitative work. This destroyed the 'middle-class' condition which a relatively large portion of the white proletariat held, it *re-proletarianized* them, as Noah Khrachvik argues.[36]

Therefore, as I have previously stated,

> Works like *One-Dimensional Man*, which take upon the task of criticizing and equating 'both sides,' do the work of one side – capitalism – in creating a 'left' campaign of de-legitimizing socialist experiments. This process of creating a *'left' de-legitimation* campaign is central for the legitimation of capital.[37]

---

[35] For more on the effects of the overthrow of the Soviet Union see: Parenti's *Blackshirts and Reds*; Carlos Martinez's *The End of the Beginning*; and Roger Keeran and Thomas Kenny's *Socialism Betrayed*.

[36] Noah Khrachvik, *What is to be Done… Like Now?* (Dubuque: Midwestern Marx Publishing Press, forthcoming 2023).

[37] Garrido, "The Relevance and Failures of Marcuse's One-Dimensional Man."

The purity fetish outlook of Adorno, Horkheimer, Marcuse, and many others from the 20ᵗʰ century Western Marxist tradition, embedded within what Gabriel Rockhill calls "the global theory industry," is the ideological backdrop for their function as *"radical recuperators"* – agents of what I call *controlled counter-hegemony,* which "cultivate and market the appearance of radicality in order to recuperate potentially radical elements in society, particularly young people and students, within the pro-imperialist anti-communist fold."[38] It is no coincidence that you will only find 'Marxists' who are more critical of socialism than capitalism within the academy and media. The hegemonic order creates, finances, and proliferates *controlled counter-hegemonic* institutions, movements, and forces that channel popular discontent into areas which fail to substantially challenge the existing order. The 'Marxist' authors hailed in Western academies are but the agents through which this process of controlled counter-hegemony concretizes.

In today's context, out of the radical recuperators which continue to fashion themselves as 'Marxists,' Slavoj Žižek's "commie cosplay" has been undoubtedly the most successful in attracting people.[39] While called "the most dangerous philosopher in the West," and the world's best-known Marxist, what Žižek can actually be labeled as is the West's most efficient radical recuperator – the contemporary pope of Western Marxism's purity fetish outlook.[40] Like his anti-communist Western Marxist forefathers, Žižek considers communism – i.e., the socialist states led by communist parties – "the worst ideological, political, ethical, social (and so on) catastrophe in the history of humanity," arguing that at an "abstract level of suffering, Stalinism was worse than Nazism."[41] While claiming that Mao made a "ruthless decision to starve tens of millions to death," Žižek, as Rockhill notes, is "well to the right of the anti-communist *Black Book of Communism,* which recognized that Mao did not intend to kill his compatriots."[42] As Rockhill argues,

---

[38] Gabriel Rockhill, "Capitalism's Court Jester: Slavoj Žižek," *CounterPunch* (January 02, 2023): https://www.counterpunch.org/2023/01/02/capitalisms-court-jester-slavoj-zizek/

[39] Rockhill, "Capitalism's Court Jester: Slavoj Žižek."

[40] José Dueño, "The most dangerous philosopher in the West?" *America* (April 04, 2018): https://www.americamagazine.org/arts-culture/2018/04/04/most-dangerous-philosopher-west

[41] "'20th Century Communism' by Slavoj Žižek," *HARDtalk BBC,* accessed through Simon Gros YouTube: https://www.youtube.com/watch?v=ThTJBKYPiNo&t=153s ; Slavoj Žižek, *Did Somebody Say Totalitarianism? Five Interventions in the (Mis)use of a Notion* (London: Verso, 2001), 127-129.

[42] Slavoj Žižek, *In Defense of Lost Causes* (London: Verso, 2009), 169.

Not unlike Elvis, who notoriously rose to fame in the music industry by appropriating, domesticating, and mainstreaming music from Black communities that was often rooted in very real struggles, Žižek became a front man in the global theory industry by borrowing his most important insights from the Marxist tradition but subjecting them to a playful postmodern cultural mash-up to crush their substance, thereby commodifying them for mass consumption in the neoliberal era of anti-communist revanchism.[43]

This 'world renowned Marxist' started his anti-communist career in his former homeland, socialist Yugoslavia, in which he admits to have been "personally engaged in undermining [its] socialist order."[44] In the period before NATO's brutal bombing of Yugoslavia, Žižek would write weekly columns for *Mladina*, "a prominent weekly publication that was part of the dissident movement against the communist government," and which, according to a "long and detailed report by the Yugoslav Communist Party," was "accused of being backed by the CIA."[45] Žižek would also go on to co-found the Liberal Democratic Party, serving as one of the leading figures and making one run for president. When the US/NATO's criminal bombing (often targeting civilian sites) and balkanization of Yugoslavia began, he wrote concerning the issue in 1999: "So, precisely as a Leftist, my answer to the dilemma "Bomb or not?" is: not yet ENOUGH bombs, and they are TOO LATE."[46]

This is the same 'Marxist' philosopher who today peddles the hysterical anti-Russia propaganda stemming from the West and who urges the 'left' to support NATO's funding of fascist Ukraine, proliferating the proxy-war against Russia that is pushing humanity closer and closer to nuclear Armageddon.[47] As Nikos Mottas argued, "It is no coincidence that

---

[43] Rockhill, "Capitalism's Court Jester: Slavoj Žižek."

[44] Thomas Moller Nielsen, "Unrepentant Charlatanism (with a Response by Slavoj Žižek)," *The Philosophical Salon* (November 25, 2019): https://thephilosophicalsalon.com/unrepentant-charlatanism-with-a-response-by-slavoj-zizek/

[45] Rockhill, "Capitalism's Court Jester: Slavoj Žižek."

[46] Slavoj Žižek, "Against the Double Blackmail," *New Left Review* 234 (March-April 1999): https://newleftreview.org/issues/i234/articles/slavoj-zizek-against-the-double-blackmail

[47] Slavoj Žižek, "Pacifism is the Wrong Response to the War in Ukraine," *The Guardian* (June 21, 2022): https://www.theguardian.com/commentisfree/2022/jun/21/pacifism-is-the-wrong-response-to-the-war-in-ukraine

the charlatan who is now calling for a "stronger NATO" to defend Ukraine, is the same guy who in 1999 was an outspoken supporter of NATO's imperialist intervention and bombing of Yugoslavia."[48]

Žižek castrates the fact, the beginning of the special operations in February 24th, from the factors which led to its existence; he completely ignores NATO's broken promise to not expand eastward, which presents an existential national security threat for Russia; he ignores the 2014 Euromaidan US orchestrated coup, which, through the involvement of the Neo-Nazi Azov battalion and the fascistic Right Sector overthrew Yanukovych and put the anti-communist and anti-Russian far-right oligarch Petro Poroshenko in power, who would go on to resuscitate the Nazi, Hitler-collaborating Stepan Bandera as a national hero; he ignores that from 2014 to 2022, 14,000 mostly ethnically Russian people in the Donbass region were killed by constant shelling from the Azov Nazis; he ignores the suppression ethnic Russians and communists have faced, which spans the entire spectrum of repression, from banning the Communist Party and the Russian language to lethal violence; he ignores that the Donbass people had been asking for Russian aid since they began getting attacked in 2014, and that the communist parties of the Russian Federation, Ukraine, Donetsk and Lugansk, the most progressive forces in the region, were the ones who first called for Russian aid; he ignores that a diplomatic solution was sought by Russia since the 2014 Minsk accords, and that, as German Chancellor Angela Merkel recently admitted, the West never sought to fulfil their promises, and instead, used the Minsk accords to buy enough time for NATO to build up Ukraine's military for their proxy war against Russia.[49] Only when this context is ignored does Žižek's dangerous and infantile position on the war make any sense, and only when ignorant of this context can we take him seriously on the subject.

With regards to Cuba (as well as China, Venezuela, and pretty much every other socialist experiment), Žižek couches his anti-dialectical bourgeois critiques of Cuban socialism within a reified analysis that strips the reality from its context.[50] He ignores the historical pressures of being a

---

[48] Nikos Mottas, "Slavoj Žižek, an apologist of Capitalism disguised as "Marxist philosopher," *Midwestern Marx Institute for Marxist Theory and Political Analysis* (July 01, 2022): https://www.midwesternmarx.com/articles/slavoj-zizek-an-apologist-of-capitalism-disguised-as-marxist-philosopher-by-nikos-mottas

[49] Scott Ritter, "Merkel Reveals West's Duplicity," *Consortium News* (December 05, 2022): https://consortiumnews.com/2022/12/05/scott-ritter-merkel-reveals-wests-duplicity/

[50] "Slavoj Žižek on Cuba and Yugoslavia," *Žižek.UK* (December 01, 2016): https://zizek.uk/slavoj-zizek-on-cuba-and-yugoslavia/

small island 90 miles away from the world's largest empire; an empire which has spent the last 60 years using a plethora of techniques – from internationally condemned blockades, to chemical attacks, terrorist fundings, and over 600 CIA led attempts on Fidel's life – to overthrow the Cuban revolution.[51] Only in ignoring this context and how it emerges can Žižek come to the purist and anti-dialectical conclusion that the revolution failed and that the daily life of Cubans is reducible to "inertia, misery, escapism in drugs, in sex, [and] pleasures."[52] Here the aforementioned paradox can be clearly seen – Cuba is too 'impure' to support, they don't measure up to his pure socialism; however, the US, NATO, and the Nazi friendly fascist state of Ukraine are not 'impure' enough to support against the Russian menace, a 'menace' which is supported by the former colonized countries (those without US puppet governments at least) and by the contemporary socialist camp.

It is also interesting to note the limits Western liberalism sets to 'acceptable' discourse. Žižek, whose resume could show nothing more than his anti-communism and opportunist 'commie cosplay,' was the one selected to represent the 'Marxist' position in a 2019 debate with Jordan Peterson on the question of happiness. The controlled counter-hegemonic institutions of the capitalist ruling class are perfectly fine with allowing an abstractly formulated anti-communist 'Marxism' on the debate stage. In so far as the myth that 'socialism has always failed' is sustained as an unquestioned and unquestionable assumption, this purity fetish compatible 'Marxism' is allowed free reign in the academy, media, NGO, and civil society in general.

Lessons from Parenti and Losurdo: Left-Anticommunism and the Fetish for Defeat

Similar positions on questions regarding the anti-colonial struggles in Asia and Africa, the Soviet Union, the DPRK, Nicaragua, Cuba, Venezuela, and other successful socialist and communist projects are taken by

---

[51] Carlos L. Garrido, "Anti-Government Protests in Cuba Provoked by U.S. Embargo Has Right-Wingers Salivating at the Prospect of Regime Change," *Covert Action Magazine* (August 12, 2021): https://covertactionmagazine.com/2021/08/12/anti-government-protests-in-cuba-provoked-by-u-s-embargo-has-right-wingers-salivating-at-the-prospect-of-regime-change/
[52] "Slavoj Žižek on Cuba and Yugoslavia," *Žižek.UK*

celebrated Western Marxists like Ernst Bloch, Kevin Anderson, Alain Badiou, and others, who always function as the left-wing of imperialism when the drums of war start playing.[53] This is the sort of 'Marxism' that imperialism appreciates, the type which CIA agent Thomas Braden called the "compatible left."[54] This is the 'Marxism' which functions as the vanguard of controlled counter-hegemony.

This is the left that Michael Parenti calls *left-anticommunism* in his book *Blackshirts and Reds*.[55] For these left-anticommunists, the communists that exist in the real world are just power-hungry 'Stalinists' which are no different, or perhaps worse, than the current capitalist order. But, as Parenti rightly notes,

> If true, one wonders why, in country after country, these Reds side with the poor and powerless often at great risk and sacrifice to themselves, rather than reaping the rewards that come with serving the well-placed.[56]

The "left-McCarthyism" of these 'socialists' "tolerate nothing less than a blanket condemnation of the Soviet Union as a Stalinist monstrosity and a Leninist moral aberration."[57] Any potential for a nuanced (i.e., dialectical) assessment of socialist experiments, or for why experiments like the USSR were successfully overthrown, is tossed out the window. Yet, they want to sustain socialism as a 'pure' ideal that, because to them it has never really been tried, hasn't been desecrated by the meanness of reality. "Real socialism," they argue, "would be controlled by the workers themselves through direct participation instead of being run by Leninists, Stalinists, Castroites, or other ill-willed, power-hungry, bureaucratic cabals of evil men who betray revolutions."[58] Unfortunately for them, as Parenti eloquently notes,

---

[53] It would be beyond the scope of this work to elaborate any more on these details. For more, I would point the reader to Losurdo's *Western Marxism* and to Rockhill's "The CIA and the Frankfurt School's Anti-Communism;" "The CIA Reads French Theory;" "Foucault: The Faux Radical;" and "Foucault, Anti-Communism and the Global Theory Industry," all found in *Philosophical Salon*.
[54] Thomas W. Braden, "I'm Glad the CIA Is 'Immoral,'" *Saturday Evening Post* (May 20, 1967): https://www.saturdayeveningpost.com/reprints/im-glad-the-cia-is-immoral/
[55] Parenti, *Black Shirts and Reds,* 41-58.
[56] Parenti, *Blackshirts and Reds,* 43.
[57] Parenti, *Blackshirts and Reds,* 46.
[58] Parenti, *Blackshirts and Reds,* 50-51.

This "pure socialism" view is ahistorical and nonfalsifiable; it cannot be tested against the actualities of history. It compares an ideal against an imperfect reality, and the reality comes off a poor second. It imagines what socialism would be like in a world far better than this one, where no strong state structure or security force is required, where none of the value produced by workers needs to be expropriated to rebuild society and defend it from invasion and internal sabotage.[59]

This is the purity fetish par excellence; if reality does not measure up to the pure idea in my head, reality is itself rejected. As Losurdo argues,

This attitude, which condemns the real movement in the name of one's own fantasies and dreams, expresses contempt for the actual future and the near future in the name of the remote and utopian future, this attitude—completely foreign to Marx and Engels—deprives Marxism of any real emancipatory charge. Adopting this attitude means arbitrarily amputating the plural temporality that characterizes the revolutionary project of Marx and Engels.[60]

These Western Marxists, as Losurdo notes, fail to see the multiple temporalities in Marx and Engels' discourse on communism:

1-   The first is communism as an active struggle waged in the actual present/near future. We see this in *The German Ideology*, where Marx and Engels say, "we call communism the *real* movement which abolishes the present state of things," and in the *Manifesto of the Communist Party*, where they say that "communists everywhere support any revolutionary movement against the existing social and political conditions."[61]

2-   The second is what is called in the *Critique of the Gotha Program* the first or lowest stage of communism, which corresponds to "a political transition period in which the state can be

---

[59] Parenti, *Blackshirts and Reds,* 52.
[60] Losurdo, *Western Marxism,* 179.
[61] Marx and Engels, *MECW Vol. 5,* 49; Marx and Engels, *MECW Vol. 6* (Moscow: Progress Publishers, 1976), 519.

nothing but the revolutionary dictatorship of the proletariat."[62] Often, this stage is just called socialism.

3-   The third is what is called in the *Critique of the Gotha Program* the "higher phase of communist society," where classes have been abolished, the state withers away, and "society inscribes on its banners: From each according to his ability, to each according to his needs!"[63]

Every time communism is brought up within the body of work of Marx and Engels it falls within one of these temporalities. Instead of seeing these dialectically, that is, seeing how the process of history itself will "build a bridge between the different temporalities," Western Marxists do what any simpleton can do – measure the struggles within the first and second stages of these temporalities through the ideal of the distant third, considering the failure to live up to the third reason enough to condemn a people's struggle.[64] This infantilism is what Lenin called "pure (i.e., abstract) communism … communism that has not yet matured to the stage of practical political action by the masses."[65]

It is only natural that their purity fetish outlook also produces a fetish for defeat. Only in the defeated revolutionary struggles has the purity of their socialist Idea not been desecrated. "No surprise then," as Parenti says, "that the pure socialists support every revolution except the ones that succeed."[66] "In other words," as Losurdo puts it,

> You can only sympathize with the Chinese, Vietnamese, Palestinian people, etc., while they are oppressed, humiliated and powerless (while they are subjected to colonialist and imperialist power); and thus, a national liberation struggle can only be supported to the extent that it is defeated. The defeat and the inconclusive character of a revolutionary movement are the premises for certain exponents of Western Marxism to be able to present themselves as rebels who refuse, in any circumstance, to contaminate themselves with the constituted power.[67]

---

[62] Marx and Engels, *MECW Vol. 24*, 95.
[63] Marx and Engels, *MECW Vol. 24*, 87.
[64] Losurdo, *Western Marxism*, 179.
[65] Lenin, *CW Vol. 31*, 94-95.
[66] Parenti, *Blackshirts and Reds*, 51.
[67] Losurdo, *Western Marxism*, 159.

The revolution that wins, that develops the productive forces, the sciences and technologies, that lifts the living standard of their people, that defends itself against imperialism, that provides universal social rights to housing, food, healthcare, education, etc., but that does this through a so-called 'authoritarian' state and in certain moments with the so-called 'capitalist road' of a socialist market economy, that revolution, according to the Western Marxist's purity fetish, should be condemned and considered 'not real socialism.'

Yet, while these 'Marxists' find "any association with communist organizations morally unacceptable because of the 'crimes of communism,'" as Parenti states,

> Many of them are themselves associated with the Democratic party in [the US], either as voters or as members, apparently unconcerned about the morally unacceptable political crimes committed by leaders of that organization. Under one or another Democratic administration, 120,000 Japanese Americans were torn from their homes and livelihoods and thrown into detention camps; atomic bombs were dropped on Hiroshima and Nagasaki with an enormous loss of innocent life; the FBI was given authority to infiltrate political groups; the Smith Act was used to imprison leaders of the Trotskyist Socialist Workers Party and later on leaders of the Communist party for their political beliefs; detention camps were established to round up political dissidents in the event of a "national emergency;" during the late 1940s and 1950s, eight thousand federal workers were purged from government because of their political associations and views, with thousands more in all walks of life witchhunted out of their careers; the Neutrality Act was used to impose an embargo on the Spanish Republic that worked in favor of Franco's fascist legions; homicidal counterinsurgency programs were initiated in various Third World countries; and the Vietnam War was pursued and escalated. And for the better part of a century, the Congressional leadership of the Democratic party protected racial segregation and stymied all antilynching and fair employment bills. Yet all these crimes, bringing ruination and death to many, have not moved the liberals, the social democrats, and the "democratic socialist" anticommunists

to insist repeatedly that we issue blanket condemnations of either the Democratic party or the political system that produced it, certainly not with the intolerant fervor that has been directed against existing communism.[68]

Ressentiment and Socialist Profile-Identity

It would be difficult not to notice that the phenomenon of *ressentiment*, i.e., the impotence-grounded transvaluation of values (the turning of reality on its head), is also enmeshed in Western Marxism's purity fetish as an indispensable emotive component. According to the orthodox view (which was reformed by Marx and Engels in posthumously published manuscripts) where capitalism was most developed, i.e., Western Europe and the US, was where socialism was to first arrive. Yet, the first successful revolution took root in Russia (the 'weakest link') and then in China, Korea, Cuba, Vietnam, and other countries from the third world. The colonial, semi-colonial, and semi-feudal conditions in these areas forced these socialist projects to focus on developing a strong state (to defend against aggression and secure sovereignty) and the forces of production, sciences, and technology (to raise living standards and shrink global inequality).[69] In this context, Western Marxism's impotence in producing a revolution would provide fertile ground for the development of *ressentiment* against those parts of the world whose revolutions were supposed to follow the West, but who actually had successful revolutions first.

This would take place in two ways: 1) socialism would itself be thought (in line with the distant temporality) as, in the words of Merleau-Ponty, "an absolute Other."[70] This reduces socialism to being merely a transvaluation of capitalist values, instead of being the sublation of the capitalist mode of life. Again, here we see a fundamental deficiency in dialectical thinking. This simply "makes virtue out of necessity," and ends up fetishizing poverty, victimhood, and as mentioned above, defeat.[71] It is, as Max Scheler argued, simply "love for something which has features that

---

[68] Parenti, *Blackshirts and Reds*, 48-49.
[69] This reorientation of focus is clear in the transition of Lenin's writings before and after the revolution.
[70] Maurice Merleau-Ponty, *The adventures of the Dialectic*, trans. by L. Rozitchner (Buenos Aires: Leviathan, 1957), 298.
[71] Max Scheler, *Ressentiment* (Milwaukee: Marquette University Press, 2007), 46.

are the opposite of those of the hated object."[72] Against this we must re-member Deng Xiaoping's statement, "Socialism means eliminating pov-erty ... Pauperism is not socialism, still less communism."[73] And 2) since their "love for the 'small,' the 'poor,' the 'weak,' and the 'oppressed' is really disguised hatred, repressed envy ... directed against the opposite phenomena: 'wealth,' 'strength,' 'power,'" it is natural that they condemn those revolutions which have succeeded in grabbing power, strengthening the people's democratic dictatorship, and abolishing poverty and illiter-acy.[74]

The power Marxism has attained in the East highlights the impotency of Western Marxism; broiling in this impotency envy develops into res-sentiment: the success in the East, because it has been impure, is deemed a failure, the failure in the West, because purity has been sustained, is deemed a success. It is a topsy-turvy world which the Western Marxist sees.

It would be helpful to remind the Western Marxists, who claim to 'go back to Hegel,' or to a Hegelianized young Marx (as if one could take a scapula to Marx and have the cut parts survive), what Hegel says in the preface to the *Philosophy of Right*: "if theory really goes beyond the world as it is and builds an ideal one as it ought to be, that world exists indeed, but only in his opinions, an unsubstantial element where anything you please may, in fancy, be built."[75] We must also recall for them the second thesis from the young Marx, which states that "man must prove the truth, i.e., the reality and power, the this-worldliness of his thinking in practice ... The dispute over the reality or non-reality of thinking which is isolated from practice is a purely scholastic question."[76]

The purity the Western Marxists seek to keep their idea of socialism in is to the detriment of the truth of socialism itself. While socialism can be said to have proved its truth, to have become *actual*, in China, Cuba, the DPRK, etc., the purity fetish worldview in which Western Marxism's 'pure socialism' exists makes it incapable of proving its truth. Socialism for the Western Marxists is, in the words of Marx, a purely scholastic

---

[72] Scheler, *Ressentiment*, 65.
[73] Deng Xiaoping, "Building a Socialism with a Specifically Chinese Character." In *Selected Works of Deng Xiaoping Vol. 3* (June 30, 1984): https://dengxiaopingworks.word-press.com/2013/03/08/building-a-socialism-with-a-specifically-chinese-character/
[74] Scheler, *Ressentiment*, 65.
[75] G. W. F. Hegel, *Philosophy of Right* (Oxford: Oxford University Press, 1978), 11.
[76] Marx and Engels, *MECW Vol. 5*, 6.

question. They are not interested in real struggle, in changing the world, but in continuously purifying an Idea, one that is debated amongst other ivory-tower Marxists and which is used to measure against the real world. The label of 'socialism' or 'Marxism' is sustained merely as a counter-cultural and edgy identity which exists in the fringes of quotidian society. That is what Marxism is reduced to in the West – a personal identity.

In places like Cuba and China, when one calls themselves a communist, they are referring not simply to ideas that they agree with, but to actions which they take within the context of a Communist Party. To be a communist is not simply a matter of personal identification; it is a label that is socially earned by working with the masses through their representative organizations. One does not become a communist simply by learning the theory and, as Lenin urged, "assimilating the wealth of knowledge amassed by humanity."[77] Although this is indubitably important, Lenin argues, "only by working side by side with the workers and peasants can one become a genuine communist."[78] This requires communist discipline, education, ethics, virtues, and the willingness to make the construction of a new society the purpose of your life.

All of this is absent in Western Marxism, which reduces what being a socialist is to personal identification. In the era of profilicity, where, as Hans Georg Moeller and Paul D'Ambrosio argue, identity formation takes the form of profile curation, the socialist identity is most clearly seen in people's social media bios, where they mention the sort of socialism they identify with, either through the word itself or through emojis (democratic socialist rose, communist hammer and sickle).[79] In the context of the hyper-individualist West's treatment of socialism as a personal identity, the worst thing that may happen for these 'socialists' is for socialism to be achieved. That would mean the total destruction of their counter-cultural fringe identity. Their utter estrangement from the working masses of the country may in part be read as an attempt to make socialist ideas fringe enough to never convince working people, and hence, never conquer political power.

The success of socialism would entail a loss of selfhood, a destruction of the socialist-within-capitalism identity. The socialism of the West is

---

[77] [77] Lenin, "The Task of the Youth Leagues." In *CW Vol. 31*, 286.
[78] Lenin, "The Task of the Youth Leagues." In *CW Vol. 31*, 298.
[79] Hans Georg Moeller and Paul D'Ambrosio, *You and Your Profile: Identity After Authenticity* (New York: Columbia University Press, 2021).

grounded on an identity which hates the existing order but hates even more the loss of identity which transcending it would entail. This is how Western Marxism's purity fetish manifests itself in the sphere of identity formation in the age of profilicity. What matters is having the perfect bio, the perfect posts, the perfect online comeback. The conquest of political power by the working class is, in short, an existential threat for the identity-socialists of the West.

Dead in the Eyes of Hegel

Where is Hegel, in the analysis of the concrete, for the Western Marxists who appeal to him? The answer is simple; he is dead. But Hegel does not die without revenge. They too are dead in the eyes of Hegel. Their anti-dialectical lens of interpreting the material world in general, and the struggle for socialism in specific, leaves them in the lifeless position Hegel called *Dogmatism*. For Hegel,

> Dogmatism as a way of thinking, whether in ordinary knowing or in the study of philosophy, is nothing else but the opinion that the True consists in a proposition which is a fixed result, or which is immediately known.[80]

Western Marxist dogmatists fetishize binaries, abstract facts, and the pure. To them, something is either socialism (if it is pure) or not-socialism (if it is impure). They cannot grapple, in practice at least, with the concept of becoming, that is, with the reality of the *construction of socialism*. Socialism must be constructed, it is an active enterprise immersed necessarily in a world riddled by imperialist pressures, contradictions, and violence – both active and passive. Western Marxists, like Marcuse, will write splendid critiques of positivism's fetish of the 'fact,' but in their own practical analysis of socialist construction in the world they too castrate facts from the factors that allowed them to exist. Their outlook is dominated by an anti-dialectical purity fetish, grounded in ressentiment, and expressing itself in a variety of ways, one of which is the paradox of socialist profile-identity.

---

[80] Hegel, *Phenomenology of Spirit*, 23.

III – China and the Purity Fetish of Western Marxism

The stakes of the imperialist West's New Cold War against China are as great as they can get. This means that the Western left's role as controlled counter-hegemony and left-wing delegitimizers of socialist states – a role ideologically grounded in their purity fetish outlook – is as dangerous as it can get. In our current geopolitical climate, all progressive forces in the West should unite against the US and NATO's anti-China rhetoric and actions. Unfortunately, what we find from large portions of this Western left is parroting of state-department narratives on China with radical-sounding language. Leading 'socialist' outlets in the US often echo baseless ruling class propaganda such as the 'Uyghur genocide,' Zero Covid authoritarianism, Belt and Road imperialism, debt trapping, and other similar fabrications.[1] Far from a concrete-dialectical study of China, in many of these spaces the claims of the ruling class are just assumed to be true, and anyone who dares to question them – and henceforth, bring the real truth to light – is labeled a puppet of Xi Jinping and the 'CCP' (which, like the Western bourgeoisie, is continuously labeled by these 'socialists' as CCP and not CPC in order to play on CCCP fears from the last cold war).[2]

Most of these tactics center on age-old claims of communist 'authoritarianism,' 'totalitarianism,' and all other such words used to equate fascism with communism and judge 'democracy' according to Western liberal-bourgeois standards. These assumptions and purity fetish engagements with Chinese socialist governance blind the Western Marxist from seeing China's de facto geopolitical role as a beacon in the anti-imperialist struggle, in the Covid struggle, in the struggle for environmental sustainability, and in the struggle to *develop with* the *darker nations* which have

---

[1] See, for instance: David Palumbo-Liu, "The Ongoing Persecution of China's Uyghurs," *Jacobin* (June 2019): https://jacobin.com/2019/06/china-uyghur-persecution-concentration-camps ; Ryan Zickgraf, "A Mask Off Moment for the Left," *Sublation Media* (May 2022): https://www.sublationmag.com/post/a-mask-off-moment-for-the-left ; Ho Fung-Hong, "The US-China Rivalry Is About Capitalist Competition," *Jacobin* (July 2020): https://jacobin.com/2020/07/us-china-competition-capitalism-rivalry ; Vincent Kolo, "Biden and Xi escalate U.S.-China conflict," *Socialist Alternative* (May 2022): https://www.socialistalternative.org/2021/05/08/biden-and-xi-escalate-us-china-conflict/
[2] In "John Ross: from Trotskyism to power-worship" from the Trotskyite website *Workers Liberty*, economist John Ross and historian Carlos Martinez are smeared as 'power-worshippers' and admirers of authoritarianism for their support of China: https://www.workersliberty.org/story/2021-06-15/john-ross-trotskyism-power-worship

been kept poor by centuries of colonialist and imperialist looting, debt traps, and superexploitation.[3]

The unquestioned, purity fetish grounded, and Sinophobic assumption of Chinese 'authoritarianism' and 'lack of democracy' also prevents the Western Marxist from learning how the Chinese socialist civilization has been able to creatively embed its socialist democracy in "seven integrated structures or institutional forms (体制 *tizhi*): electoral democracy; consultative democracy; grassroots democracy; minority nationalities policy; rule of law; human rights; and leadership of the Communist Party."[4] It has withheld them from seeing how a comprehensive study of this whole-process people's democracy would lead any unbiased researcher to the conclusion Roland Boer has arrived at: namely, that "China's socialist democratic system is already quite mature and superior to any other democratic system." This is a position echoed by John Ross (and many other scholars of China), who argues that the "real situation shows that China's framework and delivery on human rights and democracy is far superior to the West's."[5]

The purity fetish Marxists of the West love to think about democracy in the abstract, and hold up as the pure ideal a notion of democracy which is only quantitatively different from the bourgeois notion. Then, this ideal notion of bourgeois democracy is measured up against the atrocity propaganda riddled caricature of socialist states which their ruling classes paint – and they unquestioningly accept. When the caricature of reality fails to measure up to the ideal, reality – which they have yet to engage with – is condemned. What the Western Marxist forgets – thanks to the purity fetish and their social chauvinism – is that in societies divided by class antagonisms we can never talk about 'pure democracy,' or abstract democracy in general; we must always ask - as Lenin did – "democracy for *which class*?"[6] The 'democracy' and 'democratic freedoms' of capitalist to exploit and oppress will always be detrimental to working and oppressed peoples. Only an all-people's democracy (a working and popular classes' democratic-dictatorship) can be genuinely democratic, for it is the only time 'power' (*kratos*) is actually in the hands of 'common people' (*dēmos*).

---

[3] Vijay Prashad, *The Darker Nations* (New York: The New Press, 2008).
[4] Roland Boer, "We need to talk more about China's socialist democracy," *Friends of Socialist China* (September 2021): https://socialistchina.org/2021/09/26/roland-boer-we-need-to-talk-more-about-chinas-socialist-democracy/
[5] John Ross, "Democracy and policies in China far greater than the west," *China Daily* (December 2021): https://global.chinadaily.com.cn/a/202112/09/WS61b169c6a310cdd39bc7a4f6.html
[6] V. I. Lenin, *Collected Works Vol. 28* (Moscow: Progress Publishers, 1974), 249.

To claim – as American capitalists, their puppet politicians and lapdog media, and their controlled counter hegemonic 'socialists' do   that the US is a 'beacon of democracy,' and China an 'authoritarian one-party system,' is to hold on to a delusional topsy turvy view of reality.[7] If democracy is considered from the standpoint of the capitalist's ability to arbitrarily exert their will on society at the expense of working people and the planet, then, of course, the US is a beacon of *this* form of so-called 'democracy,' and China an 'authoritarian' regime that stands in the way of this 'freedom.' If instead, democracy is considered from the standpoint of common people's ability to exert their power successfully over everyday affairs – that is, if democracy is understood in the people-centered form it etymologically stands for – then it would be indisputable that China is far more democratic than the US (and any other liberal-bourgeois 'democracy').

However, the object of this text is not to address and 'debunk' all the assertions made about China (or any other socialist country) from the Western left – specifically the Trotskyites and the Democratic Socialists. That would, for one, require a much more expansive project, and two, is a task that has already been done many times before. Projects like *Friends of Socialist China* and *Qiao Collective* consistently engage in the practice of debunking the propaganda on China proliferated by the Western ruling class and the 'left.' The objective of this text is different; it seeks not only to point out falsities in the Western left's positions, but to understand the worldview which consistently reproduces these. I have called this worldview the purity fetish. In it we can find the ideological roots for the Western Marxist positions on China.

In the Western Marxist's purity fetish assessment of China, it is held that because China doesn't measure up to the pure socialist Ideal in their heads, because China does not have, as Samir Amin notes, "the communism of the twenty-third century," – it is *not actually socialism*.[8] The question of democracy and authoritarianism has already been assessed in previous chapters – it is a classic of the Western Marxist condemnation toolbox. My focus in this chapter will be on those who claim China is 'capitalist' because it developed private ownership and markets with the period of Reform and Opening Up in 1978. This form of the purity fetish centers on their inability to understand, in a dialectical manner, how markets and private property function within China's socialism. China,

---

[7]Nectar Gan and Steve George, "China claims its authoritarian one-party system is a democracy – and one that works better than the US," *CNN* (December 2021):
https://www.cnn.com/2021/12/08/china-china-us-democracy-summit-mic-intl-hnk/index.html
[8] Amin, *Only People Make Their Own History*, 110.

according to these Western Marxists, took the 'capitalist road' in 1978. As Roland Boer has shown in his article "Not Some Other -ism"—On Some Western Marxist Misrepresentations of Chinese Socialism," there are four major 'sub-forms' through which this first form of condemnation occurs: 1) capitalist socialism; 2) neoliberalism with Chinese characteristics; 3) bureaucratic capitalism; and 4) state capitalism. Often, variations of these can be found within the same critic, as none are the result of a rigorous, principled analysis.

As US and Western imperialist powers ramp up the New Cold War against China, Western Marxism's erroneous purity fetish view of Chinese socialism requires closer examination.

The Purity Fetish and The Capitalist Road Thesis

From the moment that the Communist Party of China, spearheaded by Deng Xiaoping, embarked on the process of Reform and Opening Up in 1978, the Western world – both the hegemonic forces and the 'socialist' critics – held that China had taken the 'capitalist road' and betrayed the revolution. Opening up to foreign capital to develop the productive forces and modernize was considered a betrayal of socialism and the cause of the working class and peasantry. While it is understandable how, from the perspective of an outsider, this might have seemed to be the case, this judgment nonetheless reflects a deep ignorance of the debates shaping Reform and Opening Up, of the roll that lessons from past socialist experiments played in crafting it (e.g., Lenin's New Economic Policy, Chinese New Democracy, and Yugoslavian Socialist Market economics), and of the poverty of dialectical thinking present in their purity fetish outlook.

Reform and Opening Up did not come out of a void; Deng did not just wake up one day and voluntaristicly say, "let's do this!" Instead, there were objective forces which made Reform and Opening Up the most viable route for the Chinese revolution to embark on. "Thirty-five years ago," as Yi Wen writes, "China's per capita income was only one-third of that of sub-Saharan Africa."[9] Justin Yifu Lin, former chief economist and senior vice president of the World Bank, writes that "an estimated 30 percent of rural residents, about 250 million [people], lived below the poverty line,

---

[9] Yi Wen, "China's Rapid Rise: From Backward Agrarian Society to Industrial Powerhouse in Just 35 Years," *Federal Reserve Bank of St. Louis* (April 11, 2016): https://www.stlouisfed.org/publications/regional-economist/april-2016/chinas-rapid-rise-from-backward-agrarian-society-to-industrial-powerhouse-in-just-35-years#authorbox

relying on small loans for production and state grants for food."[10] In a 1979 speech Deng notes that

> China is still one of the world's poor countries. Our scientific and technological forces are far from adequate. Generally speaking, we are 20 to 30 years behind the advanced countries in the development of science and technology.[11]

China was, in short, still a very poor country, and one excluded from the developments of the rest of the world by the forces of imperialism. As Carlos Martinez notes, "China in 1978 remained backwards in many ways ... the bulk of the population lived in a very precarious existence, many without access to modern energy and safe water ... China's per capita income was $210, [and] food production, and consequently average food consumption, was insufficient."[12]

The Importance Marxism Lays on the Development of the Productive Forces

These conditions made the construction of socialism increasingly difficult, and, if allowed to continue, could have created fertile ground for national discontent in the revolutionary process. If the people's living standards continued to drag in comparison to the rest of the world, the Chinese – as many Russians did in the late 1980s and early 1990s – could lose trust in their party and in socialist construction. It was clear that a change was needed to remove the fetters preventing the development of the forces of production. The Marxist tradition has always understood that only in the development of the forces of production can socialism flourish. In *Capital Vol. I*, for instance, Marx writes that:

> The development of society's productive forces... [create the]... material conditions of production which alone can form the real basis of a higher form of society, a society in which the full

---

[10] Justin Lifu Yin, *Demystifying the Chinese Economy* (Cambridge: Cambridge University Press, 2012), 6.
[11] Deng Xiaoping, "Uphold the Four Cardinal Principles (1979)," *Selected Works of Deng Xiaoping*: https://dengxiaopingworks.wordpress.com/2013/02/25/uphold-the-four-cardinal-principles/
[12] Carlos Martinez, *No Great Wall: On the Continuities of the Chinese Revolution* (Carbondale: Midwestern Marx Publishing Press), 25.

and free development of every individual forms the ruling principle.[13]

It is the development of "the material conditions and the social combination of the process of production" which "ripens," in the capitalist mode of life, "both the elements for forming a new society and the forces tending towards the overthrow of the old one."[14] As with other modes of life, Marxist have long understood that capitalist relations of production, while at one point being "forms of development [for] the productive forces," have in time "turn[ed] into their fetters."[15] Socialist relations of production have always been understood to have the capacity of breaking through these fetters and helping unleash the forces of production. As Marx famously writes in *Capital Vol. I.,*

> The monopoly of capital becomes a fetter upon the mode of production, which has sprung up and flourished along with, and under it. Centralization of the means of production and socialization of labour at last reach a point where they become incompatible with their capitalist integument. Thus integument is burst asunder. The knell of capitalist private property sounds. The expropriators are expropriated.[16]

A similar argument is made by Engels in his celebrated *Socialism: Utopian and Scientific:*

> The expansive force of the means of production bursts asunder the bonds imposed upon them by the capitalist mode of production. Their release from these bonds is the sole prerequisite for an unbroken, ever more rapidly advancing development of the productive forces, and thus of a practically unlimited growth of production itself.[17]

In his "Critique of the Gotha Program," while elaborating on some general characteristics and preconditions for the highest phase of communist society, Marx would say that,

---

[13] Karl Marx, *Capital Vol I.,* (London: Penguin, 1982), 739.
[14] Marx, *Capital Vol I.,* 635.
[15] Karl Marx, *A Contribution to the Critique of Political Economy* (New York: International Publishers, 1999), 21.
[16] Marx, *Capital Vol. I.,* 929.
[17] Friedrich Engels, *Socialism: Utopian and Scientific* (Chicago: Revolutionary Classics, 1993), 109.

> In the highest phase of communist society, after the enslaving subordination of the individual to the division of labour, and therewith also the antithesis between mental and physical labour, has vanished; after labour has become not only a means of life but life's prime want; after *the productive forces have also increased with the all-round development of the individual*, and all the *springs of cooperative wealth flow more abundantly* – only then can the narrow horizon of bourgeois right be crossed in its entirety and society inscribe on its banner: From each according to his ability, to each according to his needs![18]

Capitalist relations of production in time become a barrier for human progress – both in the forces of production, i.e., the economic base of society, but also in culture, politics, arts, philosophy i.e., the superstructure of society. While more progressive than the feudal orders which preceded it in Europe, capitalism produces an enormous waste. It wastes labor, human potential, nature, and everything in between. As British socialist William Morris eloquently stated, "The truth is that our system of Society is essentially a system of *waste*."[19] Not only would socialist relations of production remove the artificial fetters created by a society wherein production is aimed at profit, but also the extreme wastefulness in labor, life, and things created by such anarchic production for-profit. As Engels argues,

> The social appropriation of the means of production puts an end not only to the current artificial restrictions on production [i.e., capitalist fetters], but also to the positive waste and devastation of productive forces and products… It sets free for the community at large a mass of means of production and products by putting an *end to the senseless luxury and extravagance of the present ruling classes and their political representatives*. [This affords] the possibility of securing for every member of society, through social production, an existence which is not only perfectly adequate materially and which becomes daily richer, but also guarantees him the completely free development and exercise of his physical and mental faculties.[20]

---

[18] Marx and Engels, *MECW Vol. 24*, 87.
[19] William Morris, "As to Bribing Excellence," *William Morris Archive*: http://morrisarchive.lib.uiowa.edu/items/show/2322.
[20] Engels, *Socialism: Utopian and Scientific*, 109.

The emphasis on the development of the forces of production has led critics of Marxism to argue that socialism would reproduce the same 'productivism' as capitalist society. This depicts a fundamental poverty of dialectical thinking. Yes, socialism seeks to unleash the productive forces and create the sort of abundance wherein the human community can "leap from the kingdom of necessity into the kingdom of freedom."[21] However, this growth is people-centered, not capital-centered. The aim of the development of the forces of production is not the accumulation of endless profit in a small group of hands. Far from this capitalist *telos*, which grows without regard for nature and human life, socialist growth is centered on creating conditions for the greatest amount of human flourishing – something which necessarily implies de-alienating humans from nature and overcoming the *metabolic rifts* capitalist production unquestionably creates.[22]

Instead of carrying out production in environmentally unsustainable ways – as capitalism does – socialist production allows for both developments in the productive forces and – because of its efficiency and momentum towards the elimination of superfluous waste – for this development to be carried out in a metabolic harmony with nature. As Marx argues in *Capital Vol. III.*, communist production would

> Govern the human metabolism with nature in a rational way, bringing it under collective control instead of being dominated by it as a blind power; accomplishing it with the least expenditure of energy and in conditions most worthy and appropriate for their human nature.[23]

This harmonious metabolism, or balance, can be seen most clearly in China's efforts to build a socialist ecological civilization – a task it embarked on at the 17th National Congress of the Communist Party of China (CPC) in 2007. As it reads in the latest update to the CPC's constitution, following the 20th National Congress of the CPC in 2022, the Party must

---

[21] Engels, *Socialism: Utopian and Scientific,* 110.

[22] Capitalism "produces conditions that provoke an irreparable rift in the interdependent process of social metabolism, a metabolism prescribed by the natural laws of life itself." Karl Marx, *Capital Vol. III* (London: Penguin, 1991), 949. For more see John Bellamy Foster's work, especially *Marx's Capital* and *The Return of Nature*, and Ian Agnus's work, especially *Facing the Anthropocene* and *The War against the Commons: Dispossession and Resistance in the Making of Capitalism.*

[23] Karl Marx, *Capital Vol III*, 958-9.

"work to balance … relations between humankind and nature."[24] "Harmony between humankind and nature," as the constitution argues, is a fundamental component "in building a socialist ecological civilization" capable of creating "a positive path to development that ensures increased production, higher living standards, and healthy ecosystems."[25] This dialectic of *sustainable development*, central to Marx and Engels's understanding of socialism, finds its highest concrete form to date in China's efforts to construct a socialist ecological civilization. As John Bellamy Foster, who has spearheaded the movement towards emphasizing the ecological dimensions of Marx and Engels's thought, has argued: China's "developments reflect the recognition of a dialectic in this area that has long been part of Marxist theory."[26] In so doing, Foster argues, "China's role in promoting ecological civilization as a stage in the development of socialism can be seen as its greatest gift to the world at present in terms of environmental governance."[27]

Deng and Reform and Opening Up

Although the cultural revolution had come to halt in 1976, similar forms of dogmatism and book worshiping remained for some time. Hua Guofeng's two whatevers ("We will resolutely uphold whatever policy decisions Chairman Mao made, and unswervingly follow whatever instructions Chairman Mao gave"), for instance, perpetuated the sort of book worshiping which not only sucked the living spirit out of Marxism-Leninism and Mao Zedong Thought, but proved futile in dealing with the problems China faced.[28]

"The emancipation of minds," as Deng eloquently noted, was indispensable; historical conditions had developed such that many cadres, especially many leading cadres, remained fettered by rigid thinking and book worshiping.[29] Under the justification of following Mao, they would

---

[24] "CONSTITUTION OF THE COMMUNIST PARTY OF CHINA (Revised and adopted at the 20th National Congress of the Communist Party of China on October 22, 2022)," *Qiushi* (October 2022): http://en.qstheory.cn/2022-10/27/c_824864.htm 8.
[25] "Constitution of the Communist Party of China," 10.
[26] John Bellamy Foster et. al., "Why is the great project of Ecological Civilization specific to China?," *Monthly Review* (October 2022): https://mronline.org/2022/10/01/why-is-the-great-project-of-ecological-civilization-specific-to-china/
[27] Foster et. al., "Why is the great project of Ecological Civilization specific to China?"
[28] "Resolution on certain questions in the history of our party since the founding of the People's Republic of China," *Marxist Internet Archive*: https://www.marxists.org/subject/china/documents/cpc/history/01.htm
[29] Deng Xiaoping, "Emancipate the Mind, Seek Truth From Facts and Unite As One In Looking to the Future (1978)," *Selected Works of Deng Xiaoping*:

participate in the same form of book worshiping Mao urged to overcome.[30] The needs of the time, therefore, were elaborated by Deng in the following manner:

> Only if we emancipate our minds, seek truth from facts, proceed from reality in everything and integrate theory with practice, can we carry out our socialist modernization programme smoothly, and only then can our Party further develop Marxism-Leninism and Mao Zedong Thought.[31]

The process of Reform and Opening Up required the liberation of thought from the dogmatism that wanted to perpetuate more of the same. To achieve the four modernizations Zhou Enlai enumerated (initially theorized as the second stage of the third five-year plan), namely, "the comprehensive modernization of agriculture, industry, national defense and science and technology before the end of the century, so that our national economy will be advancing in the front ranks of the world," the emancipation of the mind from book worshiping and dogmatism was necessary.[32] To be able to understand the world dialectically, to seek truth from facts, the Chinese needed to emancipate the mind. With the mind emancipated, the inflexible rigidity which rejected Reform and Opening Up could be destroyed, and a new phase of development in the Chinese revolution emerge.

It must be noted that, regardless of the pre-'78 flaws Reform and Opening Up sought to overcome, it marked a new phase in the development of the Chinese revolution, not a 'break' with the pre-'78 era. There are, as Carlos Martinez notes, 'no great walls,'

> In each stage of its existence, the CPC has sought to creatively apply and develop Marxism according to the prevailing concrete circumstances; always seeking to safeguard China's sovereignty, maintain peace, and build prosperity for the masses of the people.

---

https://dengxiaopingworks.wordpress.com/2013/02/25/emancipate-the-mind-seek-truth-from-facts-and-unite-as-one-in-looking-to-the-future/

[30] Mao Tse-Tung, "Oppose Book Worship (1930)," In *Selected Works of Mao Tse-Tung Vol. 6* (India: Kranti Publications, 1990).

[31] Xiaoping, "Emancipate the Mind, Seek Truth From Facts and Unite As One In Looking to the Future."

[32] Zhou Enlai, "Report on the Work of the Government (1975)," *Zhou Enlai Internet Archive* https://www.marxists.org/reference/archive/zhou-enlai/1975/01/13.htm

> Through many twists and turns, this has been a constant of a hun-
> dred years of Chinese Revolution.[33]

Regardless of certain failures and excesses of the pre-'78 era (most no-
tably found in the Great Leap Forward and the Cultural Revolution), it was
successful in many areas, and without both its successes and failures, Reform and Opening Up could not have occurred. As Cheng Enfu has argued,
"the historical period after reform and opening-up cannot be used to negate
the historical period before reform and opening-up, and vice versa."[34] The
successes of Reform and Opening Up, as Samir Amin notes, "would not
have been possible without the economic, political, and social foundations
that had been built up in the preceding period."[35] Hu Angang writes that
"China succeeded in feeding one-fifth of the world's population with only
7 percent of the world's arable land and 6.5 percent of its water … China's
pre-1978 social and economic development cannot be underestimated."[36]
"In 1949," for instance, "the country's population was 80 percent illit-
erate," by 1978, this was "reduced to 16.4 percent in urban areas and 34.7
percent in rural areas."[37] In the first three decades of the People's Republic
of China, "the enrolment of school-age children increased from 20 to 90
percent; and the number of hospitals tripled."[38]

The successes of the pre-1978 era can be lucidly seen when compared
to India. As Carlos Martinez notes, "following independence from the
British Empire in 1947, [India] was in a similarly parlous state, with a life
expectancy of 32 … At the end of the pre-reform period in China, i.e.,
1978, India's life expectancy had increased to 55, while China's had increased to 67."[39] John Ross observes that "this sharply growing difference
was not because India had a bad record – as an increase of 22 years in life
expectancy over a 31-year period graphically shows … it is simply that
China's performance was sensational – life expectancy increased by 32
years in a 29-year chronological period - an annual average increase of

---

[33] Martinez, *No Great Wall*, 33.
[34] Cheng Enfu and Jun Zhang, "Five Hundred Years of World Socialism and Its Prospect: Interview
with Professor Enfu Cheng," *International Critical Thought* 11(1) (2021):
https://doi.org/10.1080/21598282.2021.1895508 , 17.
[35] Samir Amin, *Beyond US Hegemony: Assessing the prospects for a Multipolar World* (UK: Zed
Books, 2013), 23.
[36] Hu Angang, *China in 2020: A New Type of Superpower* (US: Brookings Institution Press, 2012),
27.
[37] "Serve the People: The Eradication of Extreme Poverty in China," *Tricontinental: Institute for Social Research* (July 2021): https://thetricontinental.org/studies-1-socialist-construction/
[38] "Serve the People: The Eradication of Extreme Poverty in China."
[39] Martinez, *No Great Wall*, 32.

2.3%."[40] This was a world-historical success, as Ross writes, "China's rate of increase of life expectancy in the three decades after 1949 was the fastest ever recorded in a major country in human history."[41] Therefore, the post-1978 successes cannot be isolated from the roll the pre-1978 successes played in laying the ground for the following phase of the revolution. "The early decades of socialist construction," as the Tricontinental Institute's report on China's poverty alleviation shows, "laid the foundation that was deepened during the reform and opening-up period."[42]

For all its successes, 1978 China was still very poor and well-behind the Western powers. It was clearly observable by the late '70s "that China's economy required an infusion of technology and capital, and that it needed to break its isolation from the world market."[43] China was beginning to suffer in ways similar to the Soviet Union in its last years. As Domenico Losurdo notes,

> the China that arose from the Cultural Revolution resembled the Soviet Union to an extraordinary degree in its last years of existence: the socialist principle of compensation based on the amount and quality of work delivered was substantially liquidated, and disaffection, disengagement, absenteeism and anarchy reigned in the workplace.[44]

The overreliance on "voluntarism and 'moral incentives' to raise production" began to "suffer from diminishing returns."[45] Like in the USSR, reforms became necessary to not lose the people.

While there are some superficial similarities between Perestroika and Reform and Opening Up, there are fundamental differences upon which the difference of outcomes is grounded. As Carlos Martinez has written, the reforms in the USSR were top-down, rushed, delegitimizing for the Communist Party of the Soviet Union and the socialist experiment's history (i.e., embedded in denigrating the party and its history – the latter of which the Chinese have labeled 'historical nihilism'); economically, privatization and marketization were carried out recklessly; key industries the

---

[40] John Ross, *China's Great Road: Lessons for Marxist Theory and Socialist Practice* (New York: Praxis Press, 2021), 17.
[41] Ross, *China's Great Road*, 17.
[42] "Serve the People: The Eradication of Extreme Poverty in China."
[43] "Serve the People: The Eradication of Extreme Poverty in China."
[44] Domenico Losurdo, "Has China Turned to Capitalism?—Reflections on the Transition from Capitalism to Socialism," *International Critical Thought* 7(1) (2017), 19.
http://dx.doi.org/10.1080/21598282.2017.1287585
[45] Martinez, *No Great Wall*, 46.

state should have sustained under its control were privatized, and the state grew less capable of commanding the economy towards the pathways which would develop, and not enervate, the revolution.[46] As Martinez notes, "given that the project was presented as a form of 'democratization,' it's ironic that it was carried out in a profoundly undemocratic manner... the leadership didn't mobilize the existing, proven structures of society (the soviets and the Communist Party) but sought to bypass and weaken them."[47]

On the other hand, the Chinese reforms were carried out in a pragmatic, grassroots, and incremental fashion – the party was never denigrated, historical nihilism was combated, key industries remained under the control of the CPC and the market activity which developed was commanded by the party to serve the ends of socialism. "Practice," as Deng said, was "the sole criterion for testing truth."[48] What succeeded in advancing the cause of socialism at the time was sustained, and what failed was abandoned. "The whole process" of Reform and Opening Up "was carried out under the tight control of the government and took place within the context of a planned economy."[49]

As Arthur Kroeber has noted, "the government will pursue reforms that increase the role of the market in setting prices, but will avoid reforms that permit the market to transfer control of assets from the state to the private sector."[50] To use a metaphor often brought up by Xi Jinping, the development of the invisible hand (the market) was not to the detriment of, but to the enhancement of, the visible hand (the state).[51] A similar phenomenon is observable with public and private ownership. As Cheng Enfu argues in *China's Economic Dialectic*, "in order to improve the ownership structure of the whole society in which public ownership is dominant and private ownership is auxiliary, it is essential to enhance the symbiosis and complementarity of the two ownerships under market competition and state orientation."[52] "The result was," as Martinez writes, "a far more effective

---

[46] See Carlos Martinez's chapter "Will China Suffer the Same Fate as the Soviet Union?" in *No Great Wall*.

[47] Martinez, *No Great Wall*, 47.

[48] Deng Xiaoping, "Excerpts From Talks Given In Wuchang, Shenzhen, Zhuhai and Shanghai (1992)," *Selected Works of Deng Xiaoping*: https://dengxiaopingworks.word-press.com/2013/03/18/excerpts-from-talks-given-in-wuchang-shenzhen-zhuhai-and-shanghai/

[49] Martinez, *No Great Wall*, 48.

[50] Arthur R. Kroeber, *China's Economy: What Everyone Needs to Know* (New York: Oxford University Press, 2016,), 225.

[51] Xi Jinping, *The Governance of China Vol. 1* (Beijing: Foreign Language Press, 2014), 128-130.

[52] Cheng Enfu, *China's Economic Dialectic: The Original Aspiration of Reform* (New York: International Publishers, 2019), 46.

programme of economic reform than that which took place in the Soviet Union from 1985-1991 or in post-Soviet Russia from 1991 onwards."[53]

The importance of not allowing economic liberalization in China to turn into political liberalization cannot be emphasized enough. In the USSR, as Cheng Enfu and Liu Zixu argue, there were three distinct categories of cause behind the fall of Soviet socialism: ideological, organizational, and political.

> Ideological Causes: "Amid the rigid theorizing inside and outside of the CPSU, and given the lack of democratic and effective education and ideological work, Khrushchev's denunciation of Stalin and the strategy of peaceful evolution followed by the West created long-term ideological chaos, which constituted the theoretical foundation and ideational precursor."

> Organizational Causes: "The large number of non-Marxist cadres that the CPSU promoted and placed in important positions led to a serious malfunctioning of systems and mechanisms that could not be put right in an effective and timely manner. The unfair and undemocratic procedures used to select members of the CPSU's leading group gradually allowed non-Marxist cadres to take over leading positions within the CPSU… Over a few years, in the name of promoting young cadres and of reform, [they] replaced large number of party, political and military leaders with anti-CPSU and anti-socialist cadres or cadres with ambivalent positions. This practice laid the foundations, in organizational and cadre selection terms, for the political 'shift of direction.'"

> Political Causes: "The CPSU leadership betrayed Marxism and socialism, a betrayal that could not be overcome using the traditional political system and its corresponding mechanisms, which were highly centralized and imposed no restrictions… In short, the group headed by Gorbachev and Yeltsin exploited the highly centralized and insufficiently regulated political system and its mechanisms in order to betray Marxism, socialism and the fundamental interests of the vast majority of the people. Here are to be found the political roots and direct cause of the dramatic changes in the Soviet Union and the countries of Eastern Europe." [54]

---

[53] Martinez, *No Great Wall*, 49.

[54] Cheng Enfu and Liu Zixu, "The Historical Contribution of the October Revolution to the Economic and Social Development of the Soviet Union—Analysis of the Soviet Economic Model and the Causes of Its Dramatic End," *International Critical Thought* 7(3) (2017): http://dx.doi.org/10.1080/21598282.2017.1355143 , 304- 306. For more on Cheng Enfu's views on

At the core of the differences in reforms between China and the USSR, and of the Soviet degeneration going back to Khrushchev, is the lack of awareness of the fundamental distinction between economic and political capital drawn out by Mao. In his 1957 speech given to the Conference of Secretaries of Provincial, Municipal and Autonomous Regions Party Committee, Mao would say that by having bought over the capitalist, the revolution has "deprived them of their political capital."[55] Here is a very important distinction between political and economic capital. Mao would say that "we must deprive them of every bit of their political capital and continue to do so until not one jot is left to them."[56] The development of capital, controlled under the people's democratic dictatorship, "serves the purpose" of developing the productive forces and "of clearing a still wider path for the development of socialism."[57] As Domenico Losurdo has eloquently noted,

> It is, therefore, a matter of distinguishing between the economic expropriation and the political expropriation of the bourgeoisie. Only the latter should be carried out to the end, while the former, if not contained within clear limits, risks undermining the development of the productive forces. Unlike 'political capital,' the bourgeoisie's economic capital should not be subject to total expropriation, at least as long as it serves the development of the national economy and thus, indirectly, the cause of socialism.[58]

Whereas the leadership of the CPSU betrayed "socialism, the party and the people" and put capital in the driver's seat, the CPC used (and uses) capital to enhance and develop socialism, the party, and the people.[59] Reform and Opening Up has not undone the expropriation of political capital from the capitalists. Regardless of how developed capital has become in China, it has been restricted from political capital. In China, political capital is monopolized in the hands of the Party and the people. It is a people's

the subject of the Soviet collapse see: Cheng Enfu and Jun Zhang, "Five Hundred Years of World Socialism and Its Prospect: Interview with Professor Enfu Cheng," *International Critical Thought* 11(1) (2021): https://doi.org/10.1080/21598282.2021.1895508

[55] Mao Tse-Tung, "Talks at a Conference of Secretaries of Provincial, Municipal and Autonomous Regions Party Committees," In *Selected Works of Mao Tse-Tung Vol 5* (Peking: Foreign Language Press, 1977), 357.

[56] Mao, *Selected Works Vol. 5,* 357.

[57] Mao, *Selected Works Vol. 5,* 357.

[58] Losurdo, "Has China Turned to Capitalism?, 18-19.

[59] Enfu and Zixu, "The Historical Contribution of the October Revolution," 306.

democratic dictatorship which uses capital to serve its needs, not the other way around. By sustaining the dictatorship of the proletariat (people's democratic dictatorship), China has not only secured itself from the crumbling fate of the USSR, but has been able to develop into the global beacon of socialism leading the modern world against US/NATO unipolar hegemony.

This distinction was well understood by Deng, who argued that "if China allowed bourgeois liberalization, there would inevitably be turmoil … we would accomplish nothing, and our principles, policies, line and three-stage development strategy would all be doomed to failure."[60] All throughout Reform and Opening Up, even in the most difficult of times (e.g., the 'Wild 90s') the four cardinal principles have been upheld: 1) We must keep to the socialist road; 2) We must uphold the dictatorship of the proletariat; 3) We must uphold the leadership of the Communist Party; 4) We must uphold Marxism-Leninism and Mao Zedong Thought.[61]

Reform and Opening Up developed as a necessary phase in the Chinese revolutionary process, wherein an overly centralized economy, combined with imperialist-forced isolation from the world, stifled development and necessitated reforms which would allow China to develop its productive forces, absorb the developments taking place in science and technology from the West, and ultimately, protect its revolution. Far from being a 'betrayal of socialism,' as the Western Marxist holds, Reform and Opening Up *saved* socialism. Not just in China, but – as China's current geopolitical role makes clear – in the world.

What Western Marxists Fail to Understand Thanks to the Purity Fetish

At the height of the carnage of the first imperialist World War, Karl Kautsky, the representative of social democracy and the Second International, would sophistically blabber about how the present war was not "purely imperialist" because, in part, it contained "national" aspirations from the working masses, especially those in Serbia. By emphasizing the lack of a "pure imperialism," and by seeing the Serbian national bourgeois

---

[60] Deng Xiaoping, "We Must Adhere To Socialism and Prevent Peaceful Evolution Towards Capitalism (1989)," *Selected Works of Deng Xiaoping*: https://dengxiaopingworks.word-press.com/2013/03/18/we-must-adhere-to-socialism-and-prevent-peaceful-evolution-towards-capitalism/

[61] Deng Xiaoping, "Uphold Four Cardinal Principals (1979)," *Selected Works of Deng Xiaoping*: https://dengxiaopingworks.wordpress.com/2013/02/25/uphold-the-four-cardinal-principles/

struggle in a reified manner, isolated from the context of the imperialist war, Kautsky was setting the grounds for his social chauvinist and right opportunist support for the war. Lenin would magnificently reply to this by saying that,

> In the present war the national element is represented *only* by Serbia's war against Austria. It is only in Serbia and among the Serbs that we can find a national-liberation movement of long standing, embracing millions, 'the masses of the people,' a movement of which the present war of Serbia against Austria is a 'continuation.' If this war were an isolated one, i.e., if it were not connected with the general European war, with the selfish and predatory aims of Britain, Russia, etc., it would have been the *duty* of all socialists to desire the success of the Serbian *bourgeoisie* as this is the only correct and absolutely inevitable conclusion to be drawn from the national element in the present war.
>
> *However*, Marxist dialectics, as the last word in the scientific-evolutionary method, *excludes any isolated examination of an object, i.e., one that is one-sided and monstrously distorted.*[62]

The absence of dialectical thinking in Kautsky is apparent in his reified assessment of the Serbian national struggle. Because this national struggle, in his eyes, desecrates the purity of the imperialist war, the ground is set for supporting imperialism under the guise of supporting national liberation. The reality, of course, is that the first imperialist war was a conflict between the great imperialist powers for the division of the world. Far from being a national liberation war, it was a war amongst empires fighting to colonize greater and greater parts of the world. The absence of dialectical thought in Kautsky, embedded within his social chauvinism and right opportunism, leads him to support the imperialist war for reasons completely contrary to what the war actually represented. Enslavement is dressed up by Kautsky's sophistry in the garbs of emancipation.

By expecting a 'pure' imperialism, the 'impurity' Kautsky observes opens the door for supporting imperialism. But for a dialectician, to expect purity out of any phenomenon in life is to resign oneself to falsity, to misunderstanding the world. As Lenin would eloquently respond,

> There are no 'pure' phenomena, nor can there be, either in Nature or in society—that is what Marxist dialectics teaches us, for

---

[62] Lenin, *Collected Works Vol. 21*, 235.

dialectics shows that the very concept of purity indicates a certain narrowness, a one-sidedness of human cognition, which cannot embrace an object in all its totality and complexity. There is *no 'pure' capitalism in the world*, nor can there be; what we *always find is admixtures* either of feudalism, philistinism, or of something else.[63]

Like all phenomena in nature and human thought, every historically constituted mode of production is heterogeneous, that is, it is never *purely* one – the dominant – mode of production, but always contains auxiliary forms of production inherited from the past and transformed in light of the new conditions. This is a position very clear in Marx's writings, which holds not only true for the mode of production (i.e., the economic base), but also for the juridical, philosophical, and political superstructures. As Marx writes in the *Grundrisse*, "in all forms of society there is one specific kind of production which predominates over the rest, whose relations thus assign rank and influence to the others."[64] Marx also observes this at play in the difference interest bearing capital in capitalism has with usurer's capital in pre-capitalist production:

> What distinguishes interest-bearing capital – in so far as it is an essential element of the capitalist mode of production – from usurer's capital is by no means the nature or character of this capital itself. It is merely the altered conditions under which it operates, and consequently also the totally transformed character of the borrower who confronts the money-lender.[65]

A similar activity, once it is embedded in a different, more developed social totality, functions in accordance with the new totality of social relations it is in. This is nothing new, it is simply a law of dialectics, and hence, of the movement and interconnection of all things. This law is called the negation of the negation (or sublation, and in German, aufhebung), and it describes the processes wherein the old is simultaneously *canceled and preserved* while being *elevated* into something new. Usurer's capital, for instance, is the *universal* which is *reconcretized in a sublated form* as interest bearing capital in the *particular*, i.e., in the capitalist mode of production. Without a proper understanding of dialectics, in other words,

---

[63] Lenin, *Collected Works Vol 21.*, 236.
[64] Marx, *Grundrisse*, 106-107.
[65] Marx, *Capital Vol. III*, 600

without a concrete understanding of the world, the important differences created by a change in context is obscured and treated one-sidedly.

Whereas Kautsky would use the 'impurity' of imperialism to support it, today's Western Marxists use the 'impurity' of socialism in China to condemn it. China's economy is not purely dominated by public ownership and distribution is not purely controlled by state central planning; private ownership plays an auxiliary role and state central planning is dialectically enmeshed with the socialist market economy. These 'impurities' are used by the Western Marxist to condemn China for *not being actually socialist*, i.e., not living up to their purity fetish mediated idea of what socialism entails. In both cases, the expectation of purity is fundamental for positions which ultimately side with imperialism. In other words, in both cases the purity fetish is a fundamental ideological component for 'Marxists' turning their backs on emancipatory movements in the global south and siding with the imperialist core.

Holding purity as the standard in judgment, as we learn from Lenin and Marx, is fundamentally mistaken – it divorces one from truth and often, thanks to a one-sided and topsy-turvy interpretation of world affairs, leads one to side with the exploiters against the exploited. The Western Marxists, genealogically rooted in the eclecticism, right opportunism, and purity fetish thought of the Second International, make the same (and worse) mistakes in their assessments of China today. In prominent thinkers such as Slavoj Žižek, David Harvey, Maurice Meisner and many others, post-'78 China is described through a dualist paradigm which reduces its economy to being 'capitalist' (because of the auxiliary role of private ownership and the market) and its state to being 'authoritarian' (because of the failure to live up to the standard of 'democracy' in the liberal West). Out of this framework a plethora of terminological conjunctures, such as capitalist socialism, bureaucratic capitalism, neoliberalism "with Chinese characteristics," and state capitalism, have arisen to re-classify and condemn China.[66] Bureaucratic capitalism and state capitalism, of course, are not new – these have a long history of being used by Trotskyites and others in the compatible left to condemn the USSR.

What is common to all of these descriptions is a failure of dialectical thought – an inability to observe China's construction of socialism as an ongoing process which will contain – as all things in the world do – internal contradictions which drive its development. In short, what is common in these descriptions (and others) is the purity fetish outlook with which China is examined. If their pure standard of what a socialist economy is

---

[66] For a more detailed account, see Roland Boer "Not Some Other Ism."

supposed to be (absolutely everything under public ownership and central planning – something not even the Soviet Union had) is not met, and if the paradigm of liberal democracy is rejected in favor of a democratic people's dictatorship, then reality must be condemned for the sake of the pure ideal; that is, China must *not actually be socialist* because it does not measure up to my Western Marxist standards and biases. Contrary to this purity fetish outlook, "a dialectical approach to modes of production," would see that "different modes of production … can be included within a dominant mode that is far from being uniform or global."[67]

The purity fetish 'Marxists' must remember what Engels said of definitions.

> From a scientific standpoint all definitions are of little value. In order to gain an exhaustive knowledge of what life is, we should have to go through all the forms in which it appears, from the lowest to the highest. But for ordinary usage such definitions are very convenient and in places cannot well be dispensed with; moreover, they can do no harm, provided their inevitable deficiencies are not forgotten.[68]

In the purity fetish Marxists, Marxism, that is, scientific socialism, loses its scientific character. Things are no longer seen in their movement and interconnections, but treated abstractly and in a reified manner. Socialism becomes a rigid definition, with a series of characteristics reality must meet in order to be labeled as 'socialist.' Scientific socialism is killed with the purity fetish – for socialism is not, as Marx and Engels wrote, "a state of affairs which is to be established, an ideal to which reality [will] have to adjust itself," socialism is instead "the real movement which abolishes the present state of things."[69] For Marx and Engels, as dialectical materialists, primacy was in the *real movement of society*, not in the abstract ideal (which is, nonetheless, not rejected as a goal to strive towards).

Socialist Markets?

In V.I. Lenin's 'Conspectus to Hegel's *Science of Logic*' he states that,

---

[67] Boer, "Not Some Other Ism," 9.
[68] Friedrich Engels, *Anti-Dühring* (Peking: Foreign Language Press, 1976), 81.
[69] Marx and Engels, *MECW Vol. 5*, 49.

> It is impossible completely to understand Marx's Capital, and especially its first chapter, without having thoroughly studied and understood the whole of Hegel's Logic. Consequently, half a century later none of the Marxists understood Marx![70]

The central message in Lenin's (rather audacious) statement is this: without a proper understanding of dialectics, Marxism is bound to be misunderstood. A century later and still, Western Marxists struggle to understand Marx, and hence, to understand the world through the Marxist worldview. This is lucidly seen in their treatment of China's usage of markets, where they dogmatically accept Ludwig von Mises' stale binary which states – "the alternative is still either Socialism or a market economy."[71]

As Roland Boer highlights, already in *Capital Vol 3* (specifically chapter 36 on "Pre-Capitalist Relations") Marx shows how markets existed in the slave economies of the ancient world, e.g., Rome and Greece, and in the feudal economies of the Middle Ages. Were the markets in each of these historical periods the same? Were they commensurable to how markets exist under capitalism? No. As Roland Boer states in his book *Socialism with Chinese Characteristics*, "market economies may appear to be similar, but it is both the arrangement of the parts in relation to each other and the overall purpose or function of the market economy in question that indicates significant differences between them."[72] As Boer points out, Chinese scholars, following the analysis of Marx's *Capital Vol 3*, understand that "market economies have existed throughout human history and constitute one of the significant creations by human societies."[73] If markets, then, predate the capitalist mode of production, why would a socialist mode of production not be able to utilize them?

The essential components of a market economy must be understood in the larger socio-economic relations in which they are embedded. While the forms in which market economies show up in Greece, Rome, and the

---

[70] Lenin, *Collected Works Vol. 38*, 180.

[71] Ludwig von Mises, *Socialism: An Economic and Sociological Analysis* (New Haven: Yale University Press, 1962), 142.

[72] Boer, *Socialism with Chinese Characteristics*, 119.

[73] Boer, Socialism with Chinese Characteristics, 119. It is also important to note that this realization is common knowledge in economic anthropology since the 1944 publication of Karl Polanyi's *The Great Transformation*, where, while holding that "there is hardly an anthropological or sociological assumption contained in the philosophy of economic liberalism that has not been refuted," nonetheless argues markets have predated the capitalist mode of production, albeit usually existing inter, as opposed to intra, communally. Karl Polanyi, *The Great Transformation*, (New York: Beacon Press, 1957). 269-277.

Middle Ages appear as the historical preconditions for the capitalist mode of production, these cannot be called 'capitalist.' In so far as these market economies existed outside of the capitalist mode of production, they can be 'de-linked,' from capitalism – and hence, their potential to be used in a socialist mode of production (especially one in its lowest stages) is completely possible. The problem is that the Western Marxist's purity fetish considers, as Von Mises did, capitalism to be synonymous with 'markets,' and socialism to be synonymous with 'planning.' In reality, the institutional form of markets exists usually along with the institutional form of planning within capitalism itself – especially in its monopoly stage. To take this institutional form and reduce it to being a uniquely capitalist phenomenon is to participate in what Roland Boer and Chinese Marxists have called *economics imperialism*.[74]

As Leigh Phillips and Michael Rozworski argue in *The People's Republic of Wal-Mart*, "Walmart is a prime example" of "centrally planned enterprises" whose scale allows them to function as "centrally planned economies."[75] In fact, "almost all countries are mixed economies that include various combinations of markets and planning."[76] Does this mean that Walmart is socialist? Only a fool would say yes. What it does show is that *both planning and market institutional forms* are conditioned by the socio-economic systems they are embedded in. Walmart's planned economy is planned by capitalists to secure profits for the owners and shareholders of the enterprise. China's socialist market economy is embedded within a larger socialist socio-economic system which conditions the market towards the common good, not just towards the profits of a few.

Chinese Marxism, following upon the tradition of Eastern European socialism (Lenin's New Economic Policy, Yugoslavia's socialist market economy, etc.), and the CPC's tradition of mixed ownership and combined market and planning institutional forms (which can be traced back from the liberated areas in the 1920s to the late 1950s), was able to 'de-link' markets from capitalism and utilize them as a method (*fangfa*) and means (*shouduan*) to serve (*fuwu*) the ends of socialism, that is, to liberate the forces of production and guarantee collective flourishing.[77] If the last four decades – wherein China has drastically raised its population's living standards and lifted 800 million people out of poverty – has taught us

---

[74] Boer, *Socialism with Chinese Characteristics*, 120.
[75] Leigh Phillips and Michael Rozworski, *The People's Republic of Wal-Mart* (London: Verso Books, 2019), 16.
[76] Phillips and Rozworski, *The People's Republic of Wal-Mart,* 14.
[77] Boer, *Socialism with Chinese Characteristics*, 118.

anything, it is that China's usage of markets as a *shouduan* to *fuwu* social-ism works.

Considering the plethora of advances China has been able to make for its population and the global movement for socialism, why have Western Marxist continuously insisted that China's market reforms are a betrayal of socialism and a deviation down the 'capitalist road'? Unlike some of the other Western misunderstandings of China, this one isn't merely a case of *yixi jiezhong*, of "using Western frameworks or categories to understand China,"[78] for, if the dialectical framework and categories the Marxist tra-dition inherits from Hegel were properly applied, there would be no mis-understanding at all. Instead, it is precisely the absence of this dialectical framework which leads to the categorical mistakes.

In both Hegel and in the dialectical materialist tradition, universals are understood to be empty if not concretized through the particular. To sepa-rate the role the particular plays for the realization of the universal is to treat the universal abstractly – to disconnect it from the developments and interconnections which allow it to be *actual*. Since markets have existed throughout various modes of production, within the dialectic of universal and particular, markets stand as the universal term. There is no such thing as a 'market in general,' markets necessarily exist through a determinate – historically conditioned – form. The form the market takes is determined by the mode of production the market exists in. As an institutional form within the 'moment of exchange,' markets are determined by – and hence, reciprocally influence – the mode of production.

Markets, Boer argues, as a "specific building block or component of a larger system" are a "universal institutional form" (*tizhi*), which can only be brought into concrete existence *via* a particular socio-economic system (*zhidu*).[79] Since the particular *zhidu* through which the universal institu-tional form of a market comes into existence is a "basic socialist system" (*shehuizhuyi jiben zhidu*), the fundamental nature of how the *tizhi* func-tions will be different to how that *tizhi* functioned under the particular *zhidu* of slave, feudal, and capitalist modes of production. As Huang Nan-sen said, "there is no market economy institutional form that is independ-ent of the basic economic system of society."[80]

As was the case with the planned institutional form in the first few dec-ades of the revolution, the market institutional form has been able to play its part in liberating the productive forces and drastically raising the living

---

[78] Boer, *Socialism with Chinese Characteristics*, 13.
[79] Boer, *Socialism with Chinese Characteristics*, 122-3.
[80] Boer, *Socialism with Chinese Characteristics*, 124. Quoted from: Huang, Nansen. 1994. Shehuizhuyi shichang jingji lilun de zhexue jichu. Makesizhuyi yu xianshi 1994 (11): 1–6.

standards of the Chinese people. However, because 1) China took this creative leap of grounding the market institutional form in socialism, and because 2) Western Marxists retain an anti-dialectical purity fetish for the planned institutional form, 3) the usage of markets in China is taken as a desecration of their Western Marxist pseudo-Platonic socialist ideal. It is ultimately a categorical mistake to see the usage of markets as 'taking the capitalist road' or as a 'betrayal of the revolution.' It is, in essence, a bemusing of the universal for the particular, of the institutional form for the socio-economic system. As Boer asserts, "to confuse a market economy with a capitalist system entails a confusion between commonality and particularity."[81]

The Importance of Supporting China

Today China stands as the main global force countering US/NATO led imperialism. Its rise signifies much more than the end of US unipolarity – it marks the end of the Columbian era of European global dominance that began in 1492. Today, the rise of China goes hand-in-hand with the rise of Africa, Latin-America, and other Asiatic civilizations. Through the Belt and Road Initiative and other programs, China's development has mutually developed its international trading partners – especially those in the global South. Africa, a continent with a plethora of resources and potential, has been pillaged by the West for five centuries. It has been kept poor while its resources and people's labor made the West rich. China's rise and win-win relations with Africa has, on the contrary, helped develop African infrastructure and elevate the living standards of the African peoples.[82] While Western pundits have a frenzy over the potential of Africa taking the Chinese route, more and more African leaders are starting to see China not only as a trading partner and ally, but as a model which can help them develop and break their enslavement to Western imperialism.[83] The same is true with Latin America, the Middle-East, and the other parts of the world which European leaders see as 'the jungle.'[84]

---

[81] Boer, *Socialism with Chinese Characteristics*, 124.
[82] Ehizuelen Michael M.O., "China Helps Africa Realize its Potential," *China Daily* (July 2022): https://global.chinadaily.com.cn/a/202208/19/WS62fee07da310fd2b29e730f0.html
[83] Wade Shepard, "Why China's Development Model Won't Work In Africa," *Forbes* (October 2019): https://www.forbes.com/sites/wadeshepard/2019/10/31/why-chinas-development-model-wont-work-in-africa/?sh=3df527057afd
[84] Josep Borrell, EU foreign policy chief, said in October 2022 that "Europe is a garden. We have built a garden. Most of the rest of the world is a jungle, and the jungle could invade the garden." https://www.opindia.com/2022/10/eu-foreign-policy-chief-says-europe-is-a-garden-rest-all-is-a-

The World Bank reports that

> Over the past 40 years, the number of people in China with
> incomes below US $1.90 per day—the international poverty line
> as defined by the World Bank to track global extreme poverty—
> has fallen by close to 800 million. With this, China has accounted
> for almost 75 percent of the global reduction in the number of peo-
> ple living in extreme poverty. In 2021, China declared that it has
> eradicated extreme poverty according to the national poverty
> threshold, lifting 770 million people out of poverty since 1978,
> and that it has built a 'moderately prosperous society in all re-
> spects.'[85]

China is emerging in every category imaginable as the forefront civilization advancing humanity into a new historical stage. It has "the longest
and most extensively used high-speed rail (HSR) network in the world;"
it has developed, with maglev technology, the fastest train in the world; it
has been, over the last 40 years, by far the fastest growing economy in the
world – doing so at a speed never before seen in world-history (defying
Western economist's decades-long repeated predictions of slowdowns and
collapses); in building its ecological civilization, it has indubitably been
the vanguard in the fight against climate change; it has pushed back, over
the last few years, against US led imperialist attacks on Cuba, Venezuela,
Nicaragua, Syria, Russia, Iran, and others; in short, it has developed as the
beacon of freedom, socialism, and progress for the new world we are en-
tering into.[86]

Is it perfect? No. This is something they publicly recognize. As profi-
cient dialecticians in governance – which they call 'contradiction analysis'
over there – they understand that such perfection – such purity – is

jungle/#:~:text=On%2013th%20October%202022%2C%20European%20Un-
ion%E2%80%99s%20foreign%20policy.go%20to%20the%20jungle%20to%20pro-
tect%20the%20garden.

[85] "Four Decades of Poverty Reduction in China," *World Bank* (2022)
https://openknowledge.worldbank.org/bitstream/handle/10986/37727/9781464818776.pdf?se-
quence=4&isAllowed=y xiii

[86] Vivi, "China High-Speed Rail Network," *China Travel* (March 2022): https://www.china-
travel.com/china-trains/china-high-speed-rail-network#:~:text=China%20has%20the%20long-
est%20and%20most%20extensively%20used,two-thirds%20of%20the%20world%27s%20to-
tal%20high-speed%20railway%20networks. ; Theo Wayt, "China unveils 373-mph 'levitating' train,
fastest ground vehicle in the world," *NY Post* (July 2021): https://nypost.com/2021/07/20/china-un-
veils-373-mph-levitating-train-fastest-in-the-world/ ; "Four Decades of Poverty Reduction in
China," *World Bank* 17 ; Carlos Martinez, "China is building an ecological civilization," *Friends of
Socialist China* (November 2022): https://socialistchina.org/2022/11/23/china-is-building-an-ecolog-
ical-civilisation/

impossible. There are always contradictions to be resolved, and which, when overcome, give way to new contradictions. This is a basic law of the movement in all things in the world. But, it cannot be denied that while the American civilization train has been stopped in its tracks for decades, experiencing degeneration as the only form of change – the Chinese civilization train races towards the future at an unprecedented speed. It represents not only the advance of China and socialism – but of humanity at large. Any rational human being – let alone one who claims to adhere to Marxism – should see clearly why this is a project we must protect from the imperialist claws that seek to destroy it; the same claws that exploit and oppress us at home.

While the US encircles China with military bases and new imperialist alliances like AUKUS; while its Sinophobic politicians and media fabricate atrocity propaganda – from the 'Chinavirus' to 'Uyghur Genocide' and 'Chinese Spy Balloons' – in order to manufacture consent for a war with China which they predict taking place by 2025; it becomes the utmost duty of American socialists and communists to defend China, to expose the atrocity propaganda as just that – *propaganda* – designed to, as Michael Parenti wrote, "invent another reality."[87]

The defense of China from imperialist attacks is not a task which is disconnected from the struggles of the working class in the imperial core. On the contrary, there are a few reasons why both of these struggles should be seen as interrelated: 1) it is the tax dollars of American working people which are being used to fight wars abroad, while back at the ranch the American people's lives keep getting worse; 2) sooner or later, it will be American workers which will be sent out to fight in wars to defend a hegemonic order that keeps them poor, and systematically sends them out to die, lose limbs, and acquire PTSD fighting against people whom they have more in common with than those who sent them to war; 3) China's success is not just China's, it is the success of socialism – and this success *must* be used to debunk the American myth that 'socialism has always failed,' and to show our working class what socialism *can* achieve, even while under the boot of imperialist hybrid warfare.

If American socialists genuinely want to bring the working masses of their nation to power, they must be fierce anti-imperialists and ardent defenders of China. Overcoming the purity fetish outlook, which functions

---

[87] Courtney Kube and Mosheh Gains, "Air Force general predicts war with China in 2025, tells officers to prep by firing 'a clip' at a target, and 'aim for the head,'" *NBC News* (January 2023): https://www.nbcnews.com/politics/national-security/us-air-force-general-predicts-war-china-2025-memo-rcna67967 Michael Parenti, *Inventing Reality: The Politics Of The Mass Media* (New York: St. Martens Press, 1986), 208.

as the ideological soil these erroneous views and positions grow out of, is an absolute precondition for this struggle.

IV - The Fettering Role of the Purity Fetish in US Socialist Organizing

The United States tells the world and its citizenry that it is the best country on the planet, a place where freedom and democracy reign, and where an American dream exists which affords all the opportunity to live flourishing 'middle class' lives with white picket fence homes and two automobiles. However, for the working masses of the United States, as the great comedian and social critic George Carlin noted, "it's called the American Dream because you have to be asleep to believe it."[1] When awake, what the American masses experience is the American nightmare; lives plagued by stagnant wages, inflation, and various forms of crippling debt. In the era of an empire in decline, the inhabitants of the belly of the beast find their conditions more and more unbearable. What the American working class is experiencing is an era of comprehensive crisis which has infiltrated every sphere of the capitalist mode of life.

The Marxist position on social revolution recognizes that there are two central factors, or conditions, which must exist for a revolution to take place. The first are the objective conditions, or what is also referred to as a "revolutionary situation."[2] The second are the subjective conditions, or those corresponding to the consciousness and organization of the working masses and the vanguard party. In this section I will argue that the objective conditions for revolution are largely present in the US, and that whatever might be missing will arrive with the forthcoming general crisis of capital, expected to hit sometime in the next two years. The problem, therefore, are not the objective conditions. Instead, it is the fact that the emergence of the subjective conditions are fettered by the purity fetish which prevails in the socialist movement. Since it is the militants in this movement which are tasked with bringing the masses into the struggle for socialism, the overcoming of this purity fetish presents the precondition for a successful counter-hegemonic project. Lenin and the experience of the Bolshevik revolution shows that "the role of the vanguard fighter can be fulfilled only by a party that is guided by the most advanced theory."[3]

---

[1] George Carlin, "Life Is Worth Losing," (2005): https://www.youtube.com/watch?v=acLW1vFO-2Q

[2] V. I. Lenin, *Collected Works Vol. 21* (New York: International Publishers, 1974) 213.

[3] V. I. Lenin, *Collected Works Vol. 5* (New York: International Publishers, 1977) 370.

It is dialectical materialism, that outlook which Engels called Marxism's "best working tool [and] sharpest weapon," that can both cure the socialist movement of its purity fetish and afford it the means to realize its historically revolutionary role.[4]

Objective Conditions in The U.S.

There are a plethora of factors which, when analyzed comprehensively, can point to the existence of objectively revolutionary conditions in the U.S. "Since the late 1970s," as the Economic Policy Institute reports, "wages for the bottom 70 percent of earners have been essentially stagnant, and between 2009 and 2013, real wages fell for the entire bottom 90 percent of the wage distribution."[5] In no state of the US is the federal minimum wage ($7.25) enough to survive; even if it is raised to $15 – as the democratic socialists and other progressives have called for – the minimum wage would still not be enough for a working class family to survive anywhere in the country.[6] With stagnant wages and inflation at a 40 year high, almost 60% of Americans are currently living paycheck to paycheck.[7] Many of these people are on the brink of joining the 600,000 homeless people wandering around in a country with more than 17 million empty homes.[8] It is not surprising, in a country where there are 33 times more empty homes than homeless people, that 34 million people, including one in eight children, experience hunger while 30-40% of the U.S.'s food supply (40 million tons of food) is wasted every year.[9]

---

[4] Karl Marx and Friedrich Engels, *Marx and Engels Collected Works Vol 26* (New York: International Publishers, 1990) 383.
[5] Lawrence Mishel, "Causes of Wage Stagnation," *Economic Policy Institute* (January 06, 2015): https://www.epi.org/publication/causes-of-wage-stagna-tion/#:~:text=Since%20the%20late%201970s%2C%20wages%20for%20the%20bottom,en-tire%20bottom%2090%20percent%20of%20the%20wage%20distribution
[6] "Minimum Wage is not Enough: A True Living Wage is Necessary to Reduce Poverty and Improve Health," *Drexel University Center for Hunger-Free Communities* (2021): https://drexel.edu/hunger-free-center/research/briefs-and-reports/minimum-wage-is-not-enough/
[7] Meghan Parsons, "Report: 58% of Americans Living Paycheck to Paycheck," *Spectrum News* (September 17, 2022): https://spectrumnews1.com/ma/worcester/news/2022/06/28/more-americans-living-paycheck-to-paycheck
[8] "Homeless Population," *USA Facts*: https://usafacts.org/data/topics/people-society/poverty/public-housing/homeless-population/ ; "Homelessness and Empty Homes – Trends and Covid-19 Impact," *Self*: https://www.self.inc/info/empty-homes/
[9] "Facts About Hunger in America," *Feeding America*: https://www.feedingamerica.org/hunger-in-america ; "Food Waste in America in 2022," *RTS*: https://www.rts.com/resources/guides/food-waste-america/

As it becomes more difficult for working class Americans to survive, more and more have been forced to turn to borrowing. Currently, the average American "has $52,940 worth of debt across mortgage loans, home equity lines of credit, auto loans, credit card debt, student loan debt, and other debts."[10] Additionally, because the US is the only developed country in the world without universal healthcare, the commodification of medicine has left more than half of Americans with such crippling medical debt that many have been prevented from "buying a house or saving for retirement."[11] This same for-profit healthcare system found it unprofitable to take the measures necessary to properly prepare for the Covid pandemic, the result of which has been that the U.S., while being only 4% of the global population, accounts for more than 16% of the Covid deaths.[12] Meanwhile, socialist China has had only a very tiny fraction of the deaths found in the U.S. (0.49%) and has four times more people.

Although the U.S.'s post-WWII rise to the dominant imperialist force in the world afforded it the means to plunder its way into becoming the richest country on the planet, what one finds today is a decrepit empire with crumbling infrastructure consistently rated in the 'D' range.[13] While more than half of federal spending goes to sustaining the world's most expensive military (spending more than the next 10 countries combined), many cities in the U.S., inhabited by millions of Americans, lack access to clean drinking water.[14] Additionally, the U.S. has been experiencing a "historic decline" in life expectancy; so much so that today the average Cuban, despite six decades of illegal blockades and hybrid warfare against

---

[10] Liz Knueven, "The Average American Debt by Type, Age, and State," *Insider* (May 25, 2021): https://www.businessinsider.com/personal-finance/average-american-debt
[11] Mike Winters, "Over Half of Americans Have Medical Debt, Even Those with Health Insurance – Here's Why," *CNBC* (March 11, 2022): https://www.cnbc.com/2022/03/11/why-55percent-of-americans-have-medical-debt-even-with-health-insurance.html
[12] "Covid-19 Pandemic Death Rates by Country," *Wikipedia*: https://en.wikipedia.org/wiki/COVID-19_pandemic_death_rates_by_country
[13] "Infrastructure Categories," *2021 Report Card for America's Infrastructure*: https://infrastructurereportcard.org/infrastructure-categories/
[14] Dave Lindorff, "Your Tax Dollars at War: More Than 53% of Your Tax Payment Goes to the Military," *Common Dreams*: https://www.commondreams.org/views/2010/04/13/your-tax-dollars-war-more-53-your-tax-payment-goes-military ; Ashik Siddique, "The U.S. Spends More on its Military Than the Next 10 Countries Combined," *National Priorities Project* (April 30, 2020): https://www.nationalpriorities.org/blog/2020/04/30/us-spends-military-spending-next-10-countries-combined/ ; Robin Lloyed, "A Growing Drinking Water Crisis Threatens American Cities and Towns," *Scientific American* (September 09, 2022): https://www.scientificamerican.com/article/a-growing-drinking-water-crisis-threatens-american-cities-and-towns/

their socialist project, lives around three years more than the average American.[15]

The hardships faced by the American people are intensified by the experience of living in one of the most economically unequal societies in human history, where even by conservative numbers the "top 0.1 percent hold roughly the same share of wealth as our bottom 90 percent."[16] In the U.S., the richest 59 Americans own more wealth than the poorest half of the population (165 million people) combined.[17] While the majority of working class Americans face difficulties in meeting their everyday needs, the richest monopolists in the country, those who own what we watch, buy, and eat, have been getting richer than ever before.[18]

However, the crisis most Americans are facing is not limited to their economic conditions. It is, instead, a *comprehensive crisis* which has rippled into all spheres of life, expressing itself through profound psychological and social ills. These can be seen in the millions affected by the opioid epidemic; in the rise in violent crime rates and school shootings; and in the mental health crisis where nearly a third of American adults are struggling with depression and anxiety.[19] All of these conditions are expected to get

[15] Deidre McPhillips, "US life expectancy continues historic decline with another drop in 2021, study finds," *CNN* (April 08, 2022): https://www.cnn.com/2022/04/07/health/us-life-expectancy-drops-again-2021/index.html ; Rob Minto, "Americans Can Now Expect to Live Three Years Less than Cubans," *Newsweek* (September 02, 2022): https://www.newsweek.com/americans-can-now-expect-live-three-years-less-cubans-1739507#:~:text=In%20Cuba%2C%20life%20expectancy%20is%20now%20nearly%20three,could%20expect%20to%20live%20to%20around%2070%20years

[16] Cyndi Suarez, "With the Highest Inequality in Human History, Societies Are Ripe for Social Change," *NP* (September 22, 2017): https://nonprofitquarterly.org/highest-inequality-human-history-societies-ripe-social-change/ ; Bob Lord, "Inequality in America: Far Beyond Extreme," *Inequality.Org* (October 12, 2020): https://inequality.org/great-divide/inequality-in-america-far-beyond-extreme/

[17] Noah Manskar, "Just 59 Americans own more wealth than half the country, data shows," *New York Post* (October 08, 2020): https://nypost.com/2020/10/08/just-59-americans-own-more-wealth-than-half-the-country-data/

[18] Bruce Livesey, "As the pandemic continues, the rich are getting richer than ever before — and economists are getting concerned," *Toronto Star* (August 17, 2020): https://www.thestar.com/business/2020/08/15/as-the-pandemic-continues-the-rich-are-getting-richer-than-ever-before-and-economists-are-getting-concerned.html

[19] Azadfard M, Huecker MR, Leaming JM, "Opioid Addictio," *National Library of Medicine – StatPearls* (January 2022): https://www.ncbi.nlm.nih.gov/books/NBK448203/ ; Emma Colton, "Violent Crimes on the Rise in 2022, Following Previous Unprecedented Spike in Muders," *Fox News* (May 18, 2022): https://www.foxnews.com/us/major-cities-violent-crimes-data-murders-shootings ; Donna St. George, "School shootings rose to highest number in 20 years, federal data says," *The Washington Post* (June 28, 2022): https://www.washingtonpost.com/education/2022/06/28/school-shootings-crime-report/ ; Gaby Galvin, "Coronavirus Survey: One-Third of U.S. Adults Have Symptoms of Depression or Anxiety," *U.S. News* (May 27, 2020): https://www.us-news.com/news/healthiest-communities/articles/2020-05-27/one-third-of-us-adults-have-signs-of-

even worse with the forthcoming financial crisis, and of course, with the climate crisis and the effects it will produce in terms of migration and resource scarcity in various parts of the world.[20]

For more than a decade studies from bourgeois institutions have themselves confirmed what Marxists have known since the middle of the 19th century; namely, that "the modern state is but a committee for managing the common affairs of the whole bourgeoisie."[21] The U.S., which spreads its blood soaked hands around the world, plundering in the name of democracy, has been outed as a place where the *dēmos* (common people) do anything but rule (*kratos*). As Martin Gilens and Benjamin I. Page show,

> In the United States, our findings indicate, the majority does *not* rule—at least not in the causal sense of actually determining policy outcomes. When a majority of citizens disagree with economic elites or with organized interests, they generally lose. Moreover, because of the strong status quo bias built into the U.S. political system, even when fairly large majorities of Americans favor policy change, they generally do not get it.[22]

Far from being the 'beacon of democracy' it fancies itself to be, what the U.S. has is a "democracy for an insignificant minority, democracy for the rich," which is the essence of bourgeois democracy.[23] Or, in other words, what the U.S. actually has is an oligarchy. However, the American people, burdened by the conditions of moribund imperialism, have been catching up to the lies that pundits and ideologues disseminate to sustain bourgeois hegemony. The U.S. has some of the lowest voter turnout rates in the developed world; around 40% of the population eligible to vote does not participate in presidential elections, and in local elections this number

---

depression-anxiety-during-pandemic For a systematic critique of the 'serotonin' theory of depression and the dominant bourgeois scientific outlook see: Carlos L, Garrido, "The Failed Serotonin Theory of Depression: A Marxist Analysis," *Science for the People* (September 09, 2022): https://magazine.scienceforthepeople.org/online/the-failed-serotonin-theory-of-depression-a-marxist-analysis/

[20] Dan Weil, "Economist Roubini: 'Severe' Recession, Financial Crisis Coming," *The Street* (25 de julio del 2022): https://www.thestreet.com/investing/roubini-severe-economic-financial-crisis

[21] Marx and Engels, *MECW Vol. 6, 486.*

[22] Gilens, M., & Page, B. (2014). Testing Theories of American Politics: Elites, Interest Groups, and Average Citizens. *Perspectives on Politics, 12*(3), 564-581. doi:10.1017/S1537592714001595

[23] V. I. Lenin, *CW Vol. 26* (New York: International Publishers, 1977) 465.

increases to around 73%.[24] More than 60% of Americans are dissatisfied with the two-party system and are ready for third party alternatives, and only around 20% approve of what congress does.[25] Naturally, it is difficult to participate in a political process in which one does not feel represented. Our two imperialist parties have reacted to this immense public dissatisfaction by cracking down on voting rights and on the ability for third parties to be on the ballot.[26] In addition to this, only 11% of Americans trust the media, 90% of which has been consolidated under the control of six companies.[27] Considering the aforementioned state of the American people, it is not surprising that despite countless resources dedicated to propagandize them against socialism, more than 40% of adults have a favorable view of socialism, and amongst millennials, polls show 70% would vote for a socialist candidate.[28]

If we refer back to Lenin's pamphlet, "The Collapse of the Second International," the symptoms of a revolutionary situation are described in the following manner:

---

[24] "Why Is Voter Turnout In The United States Lower Than That In Most Developed Nations?" *World Atlas*: https://www.worldatlas.com/articles/why-is-voter-turnout-in-the-united-states-lower-than-that-in-most-developed-nations.html ; Ashma Khalid, et. al., "On The Sidelines Of Democracy: Exploring Why So Many Americans Don't Vote," *NPR* (November 18, 2018): https://www.npr.org/2018/09/10/645223716/on-the-sidelines-of-democracy-exploring-why-so-many-americans-dont-vote ; Sarah Midkiff, "Voter Turnout On The Local Level Is Plummeting. It's Time To Change That," *Yahoo!Life* (June 19, 2020): https://www.yahoo.com/lifestyle/voter-turnout-local-level-plummeting-130012607.html

[25] Christopher Ingraham, "How to fix democracy: Move beyond the two-party system, experts say," *The Washington Post* (March 01, 2021): https://www.washingtonpost.com/business/2021/03/01/break-up-two-party-system/ ; "Congress and the Public," *Gallup*: https://news.gallup.com/poll/1600/congress-public.aspx

[26] Amy Goodman and Denis Moynihan, "Voter Suppression: The Republican War on Facts, Snacks and Democracy," *Democracy Now* (May 13, 2021): https://www.democracynow.org/2021/5/13/voter_suppression_the_republican_war_on ; Howie Hawkins, "The Democrats' Third-Party Massacres," *CounterPunch* (July 15, 2022): https://www.counterpunch.org/2022/07/15/the-democrats-third-party-massacres/

[27] Benjamin Norton, "Polls show almost no one trusts US media, after decades of war propaganda and lies," *Multipolarista* (July 30, 2022): https://multipolarista.com/2022/07/30/trust-us-media-war-propaganda/#:~:text=Very%20few%20people%20in%20the%20United%20States%20trust,in%20newspapers.%20It%E2%80%99s%20quite%20easy%20to%20understand%20why. ; Ashley Lutz, "These 6 Corporations Control 90% Of The Media In America," *Insider* (July 14, 2012): https://www.businessinsider.com/these-6-corporations-control-90-of-the-media-in-america-2012-6

[28] Julia Manchester, "Majority of young adults in US hold negative view of capitalism: poll," *The Hill* (June 28, 2021): https://thehill.com/homenews/campaign/560493-majority-of-young-adults-in-us-hold-negative-view-of-capitalism-poll/ ; Stef W. Kight, "70% of millennials say they'd vote for a socialist," *Axios* (October 28, 2019): https://www.axios.com/2019/10/28/millennials-vote-socialism-capitalism-decline

What, generally speaking, are the symptoms of a revolutionary situation? We shall certainly not be mistaken if we indicate the following three major symptoms: (1) when it is impossible for the ruling classes to maintain their rule without any change; when there is a crisis, in one form or another, among the "upper classes," a crisis in the policy of the ruling class, leading to a fissure through which the discontent and indignation of the oppressed classes burst forth. For a revolution to take place, it is usually insufficient for "the lower classes not to want" to live in the old way; it is also necessary that "the upper classes should be unable" to live in the old way; (2) when the suffering and want of the oppressed classes have grown more acute than usual; (3) when, as a consequence of the above causes, there is a considerable increase in the activity of the masses, who uncomplainingly allow themselves to be robbed in "peace time," but, in turbulent times, are drawn both by all the circumstances of the crisis *and by the "upper classes" them-selves* into independent historical action. Without these objective changes, which are independent of the will, not only of individual groups and parties but even of individual classes, a revolution, as a general rule, is impossible.[29]

These conditions constitute the objective factors one can generally find in a social revolution. In essence, as Lenin later stated concisely in *Left-Wing Communism*, "revolution is impossible without a nationwide crisis (affecting both the exploited and the exploiters)."[30] We have seen in the assessment above how the American masses are suffering more than usual, and additionally, how poll after poll has shown that they are unwilling to continue to live in the old way (e.g., immense disapproval of congress and the two-party system). These conditions are developing into what Gramsci called a "crisis of authority," namely, the moment of a crisis when the "ruling class has lost its consensus [and] is no longer 'leading' but only 'dominant.'"[31] As he famously argued, "the crisis consists precisely in the

---

[29] Lenin, *CW Vol. 21*, 213-214.
[30] Lenin, *CW Vol. 31*, 85.
[31] Antonio Gramsci, *Selections from the Prison Notebooks* (New York: International Publishers, 1971), 275-6.

fact that the old is dying and the new cannot be born; in this interregnum a great variety of morbid symptoms appear."[32]

However, the masses' dissatisfaction and their inability to live in the old way does not exhaust, as Lenin noted, all the conditions for an objectively revolutionary situation; first, the masses must not only be dissatisfied with the idea of continuing to live in the old way, they must also show the willingness to act, and secondly, the ruling class must itself be shaken by the crisis and in a position where they too cannot continue to rule in the old way.

The willingness of the dissatisfied masses to act can be seen in a variety of places: from the 2020 summer uprisings, where 25-35 million Americans protested the racist police state following the murder of George Floyd; to the 2021 'Striketober' wave where hundreds of thousands of workers went on strike; to the mass unionization efforts coming from workers in Starbucks, Amazon (which is the second largest employer in the U.S.) and other industries; to the current crisis in the railroads, where the self-proclaimed 'most pro-worker president' (i.e., Biden) forced upon rail workers a contract they voted against, leading unions like Railroad Workers United to call for the nationalization of the railroads (amongst

---

[32] Gramsci, *Prison Notebooks*, 276. This interregnum which emerges in the more spontaneous and immediate moments of a crisis of authority contains both the potential for a revolutionary rearticulation of the masses towards socialism and a counter-hegemonic project, but also the potential for reaction and the fall into fascism. Some have argued that the rise of Trump and the Make America Great Again movement symbolizes such a reaction. However, every reactionary measure the Republicans (GOP) has taken could have been prevented by Democratic (DNC) governments from Biden to Obama to Clinton, and were not (e.g., roe v wade, voting rights, privatization of the economy and the roll back of workers' rights through the Taft Hartley slavery act and the 'right to work' laws within it). In fact, in many cases the DNC is as much a protagonist as the GOP. The DNC is the major force behind the funding of neo-Nazis in Ukraine; they are themselves funding the most far right parts of the republican party; they are today the favorite party of finance capital (it is undeniable that Trump was elected as a fluke in the system - but a fluke the DNC very much preferred to the milquetoast social democracy of Bernie Sanders); the DNC is the party most militantly working to make it impossible for third parties to be on the ballot, a fundamental bourgeois-democratic right; the DNC is the party of the security state, funding and proliferating the FBI, CIA, NSA, etc.; the DNC is the party that acts nice but plays mean when it comes to police violence and the militarization of our police state (for all the Black Lives Matter slogans they take up, they are continuing to EXPAND, not DEFUND, the police - which presents a threat to all poor and working class communities, especially black and Latinos which are disproportionately attacked by the police). All of these conditions show that, besides being the socially liberal wing of the imperialist machine responsible for the destruction of unions and the popular gains working people have made over decades and centuries of struggle, the DNC is as fascistic as the GOP. In fact, an argument can be made that they are MORE fascistic, for the most reactionary sectors of FINANCE capital back the democrats and their masked, sheep-dressed-wolf form of governance. As Glen Ford used to say, there is nothing about them that is 'less evil,' what they are is the more efficient evil.

other radical demands).[33] However, all of these have been spontaneous movements (some less ephemeral than others) which have been largely unable to rise to the level of revolutionary consciousness and organization.[34] They represent, nonetheless, the prime matter with which a revolutionary organization may form a successful mass struggle for power.

Have any of these conditions shaken the American ruling class? Do they find themselves unable to rule in the old way? Our response should be a resolute yes! The American empire, with its 900 bases around the world, used to be able to overthrow governments outside of its imperial sphere of influence with relative ease. In the international community, especially after the overthrow of the Soviet Union and the eastern socialist bloc, it achieved unparalleled global hegemony, only opposed in the 1990s by Cuba and the Democratic People's Republic of Korea. All things in this world, however, are in a constant state of flux, and sooner or later, it was expected that 'the end of history' would itself end, and that U.S./NATO imperialist unipolarity would be challenged. It is our era of flowering multipolarity which marks the fall of the American empire, and with it, the ability of its rulers to 'rule in the old way.'

Imperialism, it must be remembered, is not a separate political-military phenomenon governed by the set of foreign policies a nation takes. Instead, it is a stage of capitalism, where "the dominance of monopolies and finance capital is established; in which the export of capital has acquired pronounced importance; in which the division of the world among the international trusts has begun, in which the division of all territories of the globe among the biggest capitalist powers has been completed."[35] If the U.S. state, an instrument of American and transnational finance capital, is unable to internationally govern in the ways it used to – that is, if it is unable to continue the expropriation and superexploitation of the peoples of the world – this is not simply a 'foreign policy' crisis, but a crisis in the integral state.

---

[33] Larry Buchanan, et. al., "Black Lives Matter May Be the Largest Movement in U.S. History," *The New York Times* (July 03, 2020): https://www.nytimes.com/interactive/2020/07/03/us/george-floyd-protests-crowd-size.html ; Daniel Thomas, "100,000 workers take action as 'Striketober' hits the US," *BBC News* (October 14, 2021): https://www.bbc.com/news/business-58916266 ; Noam Scheiber, "A Union Blitzed Starbucks. At Amazon, It's a Slog," *The New York Times* (May 12, 2022): https://www.nytimes.com/2022/05/12/business/economy/amazon-starbucks-union.html
[34] As Lenin noted, spontaneity, "in essence, represents nothing more nor less than consciousness in an embryonic form." Lenin, *CW Vol. 5,* 274.
[35] V. I. Lenin, *Collected Works Vol. 22* (New York: International Publishers, 1974) 266-267.

From failed coup attempts in Nicaragua, Venezuela, Cuba, and other countries, to the failed 'Summits of the Americas,' to failing proxy wars against Russia and China; it becomes an undeniable fact that the ruling class cannot continue ruling in the old way, that the age of American imperialist unipolarity is over. As the world continues to turn towards China for win-win relations in international trade; as *la Patria Grande* continues its leftward turn and its hemispheric unity against the U.S.'s Monroe Doctrine style engagement with the region; as movements towards de-dollarization occur across the planet; as European citizens continue to protest the deterioration of their material conditions by the U.S. and NATO's proxy war against Russia; this crisis in the ruling class will show itself to be more pronounced.

Additionally, what greater depiction of this crisis of legitimacy than the fact that both parties, over the last two presidential election cycles, have committed themselves to challenging the results? First, with the election of Donald Trump in 2016 – a victory which was garnered while losing the popular vote – the democrats spent the next four years pushing the narrative that Trump colluded with Russia, and even attempted to impeach him over this. This, along with a long-standing history of anti-Soviet and anti-Russia propaganda, set the ideological grounds – especially amongst previously 'anti-war' liberals – for the Russia hysteria and Putin demonization driving the liberal thirst for WWIII now. Then, in 2020, the same was done by a significant portion of the republican party and by most of the MAGA base, who argued that the election was stolen by the Democrats.

As Marxists know, democracy in liberal bourgeois states is limited to the peaceful transfer of power from one faction of the ruling class to another through elections. Today, even this superficial appearance of democracy is crumbling. In doing so, we can see here another symptom of the ruling classes not being able to rule in the old way.

In essence, by every standard the Marxist tradition uses to assess objectively revolutionary conditions, the U.S. currently meets all of them – and they seem to be only deepening in the coming months and years. However, "social revolution demands unity of objective and subjective conditions."[36] As Lenin noted, "revolution arises only out of a situation in which the above-mentioned objective changes are accompanied by a subjective

---

[36] F. V. Konstantinov, et. al., *The Fundamentals of Marxist-Leninist Philosophy* (Moscow: Progress Publishers, 1982) 326.

change, namely, the ability of the revolutionary *class* to take revolutionary mass action *strong* enough to break (or dislocate) the old government, which never, not even in a period of crisis, "falls," if it is not toppled over."[37]

Subjective Conditions in the US

The development of the subjective conditions for revolution is, in essence, synonymous with the development of a successful counter-hegemonic project – that is, with the development of an intellectual and moral vanguard that can win over the masses' minds and hearts to the struggle for socialism. For Gramsci, "the starting point" of every counter-hegemonic struggle "must always be that common sense which is the spontaneous philosophy of the multitude and which has to be made ideologically coherent" by Marxist philosophy.[38] As Jean-Pierre Reed and I have argued,

> The intellectual leaders of a counter-hegemonic project will find that their theoretical weapon – the philosophy of praxis [dialectical materialism] – is null in persuading the masses insofar as it does not begin with a critical rearticulation of the popular beliefs the masses already hold. Within the incoherent, fragmentary, and contradictory clusters of beliefs which the masses hold, the intellectual leadership must find the kernels out of which socialist consciousness and emotions may develop… This educative process is comprehensive in character: the intellectual leadership does not simply wish to elevate the masses to a "higher conception of life," but to a higher *form of life* in general – it is a transformation which modifies the outlook the masses have towards the world, and, alongside this, changes the masses' desires, passions, emotions, and ethical life.[39]

---

[37] Lenin, *Collected Works Vol. 21*, 214.
[38] Gramsci, *Prison Notebooks*, 421.
[39] Jean-Pierre Reed and Carlos L. Garrido, "Intellectuals, Ideology, and the Ethico-Political," In *The Elgar Companion to Antonio Gramsci*, edited by William K. Carroll (Elgar Publishing Co., Forthcoming 2023).

For the ideological and emotive rearticulation of the masses' common sense and feelings, what is required from the intellectual leadership (i.e., the vanguard party) is a "dialectical and referential" relationship with the masses.[40] In order to successfully educate the masses, the vanguard must be grounded in them, they must learn from the masses and know them concretely. Its relationship with the masses must be "active and reciprocal," such that "every teacher is always a pupil and every pupil a teacher."[41] "The educator," as the young Marx had noted, "must himself be educated."[42]

PMC Left and Petty-Bourgeois Radicalism

This fundamental grounding in the working class is absent in the socialist 'left' of the U.S. There exists a profound gulf between the working class and socialist organizations, and what often comes to dominate in the latter is what Gus Hall called "petty bourgeois radicalism" – a mode of political practice and thinking which reflects the interests of the petty-bourgeoisie and, especially today, what Barbara and John Ehrenreich called the Professional Managerial Class (PMC).[43] We may refer to these class positions under the broader term of 'middle class.' Nonetheless, what is important to note is that the class composition of the left in the US is dominated by this middle class. This is not a new phenomenon. As Barbara and John Ehrenreich argued in the late 1970s,

> This 'middle-class' left, unlike its equivalent in early twentieth-century Europe or in the Third World today, is not a minority within a mass working class (or peasant) movement, it is, to a very large extent, the left itself.[44]

---

[40] Jean-Pierre Reed, "Theorist of Subaltern Subjectivity: Antonio Gramsci, Popular Beliefs, Political Passion, and Reciprocal Learning," *Critical Sociology* 39(4) (2012) 561–591, 565: DOI: 10.1177/0896920512437391

[41] Gramsci, *Prison Notebooks*, 350.

[42] Karl Marx and Friedrich Engels, *Marx and Engels Collected Works Vol 5* (New York: International Publishers, 1976) 4.

[43] Gus Hall, "Crisis of Petty-Bourgeois Radicalism," *Political Affairs* (1970): https://www.marxists.org/archive/hall/1970/crisis-petty-bourgeois-radicalism.htm

[44] Barbara and John Ehrenreich, "The Professional-Managerial Class," *Radical America* 11(2) (March-April 1977), 7.

Although it is perfectly fine to include professionals, managers, and part of the petty-bourgeoisie in the socialist struggle, the base of any socialist organization must be the working masses, not these other classes which, although hurt by state-monopoly capital, bring with them class biases (some which are antagonistic to the working class) into the workers movement. Marx had already warned about the negative influence professionals could bring into the labor movement, and held that the precondition for professionals to be allowed within socialist organizations must be that "they should not bring with them the least remnant of bourgeois, petty-bourgeois, etc., prejudices, but should unreservedly adopt the proletarian outlook."[45] It is impossible for these conditions to be met as the left stands today, where the PMC segment of the middle-class is the most dominant, and is composed of

> Salaried mental workers who do not own the means of production and whose major function in the social division of labor may be described broadly as the reproduction of capitalist culture and capitalist class relations.[46]

This class functions and develops its political culture through what has been called the *iron triangle* institutions of academia, the media, and NGO's.[47] Its engagements with the working class often leave the latter feeling as if they were approached by Human Resources (HR). The HR atmosphere estranges and repels working people while providing a warm home for more PMC individuals. This creates positive feedback loops that proliferate the influence of the PMC in socialist organizations. As Noah Khrachvik has argued:

> It does not matter how nice or just the petty bourgeois radical's ideas sound. It does not matter how many petty bourgeois radicals cancel the working class for not living up to [their] fantasy, or try to bully it into silence or subjugation to the lofty places the professionals and petty bourgeoisie occupy within their own minds–

---

[45] Karl Marx and Friedrich Engels, "Circular Letter to August Bebel, Wilhelm Liebknecht, Wilhelm Bracke and Others (September 17-18, 1879)," In *MECW Volume: 24* (Moscow: Progress Publishers, 1989), 268.
[46] Barbara and John Ehrenreich, "The Professional-Managerial Class." 13.
[47] Class Unity, "The Left's Middle-Class Problem."

if the class interests of the proletariat are not being fulfilled–and more, if the proletariat *does not see and understand* that its interests are being fulfilled, then there will be no revolutionary motion or movement. There will be stagnation at best, and reaction at worst.[48]

However, the dominance of the PMC within socialist organizing in the U.S. is not a spontaneous phenomenon. It is grounded on a century of state sanctioned anti-communist attacks which have purged communists from trade unions and infiltrated socialist organizations to promote factionalism and forms of socialism which are compatible with the existing order. The work of Gabriel Rockhill on the "global theory industry" shows how, through groups like the Congress for Cultural Freedom, the works of classical authors from the Western Marxist tradition were propped up by a "political economy of knowledge" that was *and is* backed by Western capitalist state departments and intelligence agencies (as well as by major capitalist foundations like Rockefeller, Ford, etc.) who benefit from the dissemination of a compatible, anti-Communist 'Marxism' which, although critical of capitalism, denounces every socialist experiment seen around the world and justifies the wars of empire from the 'left' when it needs to.[49]

Three Forms the Purity Fetish Takes in the US

1- Rejection of Actually Existing Socialism

These are the objective forces grounding the purity fetish of Western Marxism. It is not only the only 'Marxism' which is acceptable within the American academy and civil society, but it has itself become an indispensable component for the defense of the existing order. Many of the individual radical recuperators "do this," as Marx highlighted with the commodity fetish, "without being aware of it."[50] It is likely that most genuinely

---

[48] Noah Khrachvik, "Modern Petty Bourgeois Radicalism: A Tribute, Exposition, and Modern Application of the Theory of Gus Hall," *Journal of American Socialist Studies* 2 (2022), 31.
[49] For more see: Gabriel Rockhill: "The CIA and the Frankfurt School's Anti-Communism" *Philosophical Salon* (June 27, 2022); "Foucault: The Faux Radical" *Philosophical Salon* (October 12, 2020); "Foucault, Anti-Communism, and the Global Theory Industry: A Reply to Critics" *Philosophical Salon* (February 01, 2021).
[50] Marx*, Capital Vol. I*, 166-167.

consider their ideas and practices revolutionary. That does not change, however, the objective role they play for counterrevolutionary politics. Afterall, "honest opportunism," as Engels highlighted, "is perhaps the most dangerous of all!"[51] Their objective counterrevolutionary position is a natural result of the fact that, if they genuinely consider (as they do) communism to be as evil as fascism, then bourgeois liberal democracy is, like the world Leibniz's God has created, the best of all possible worlds. This makes it the ideal form of controlled opposition; an opposition that buys fully into Thatcher's TINA (there is no alternative), and hence, will never substantially oppose the existing order, for it considers the alternative far worse. From a Gramscian perspective, this shows how *controlled forms of 'counter-hegemony'* have become necessary to sustain the hegemony of the existing order; and how the dominant institutions have been able to get ahead of the discontent capitalism creates by diverting dissenters into organizations and pathways of critique which don't substantially threaten capitalist-imperialism.

This position is pervasive in the Bernie Sanders and Democratic Socialist movement which composes the largest chunk of 'socialist' organizing in the US. For instance, in the 2019 socialism conference, hosted by the Democratic Socialists of America, Jacobin, and Haymarket Books, socialist countries like China, Cuba, Venezuela, and Nicaragua were condemned as 'authoritarian.' The following week a report from Ben Norton and Max Blumenthal would show that some of the hosted panelists had received large sums of money from various imperialist organizations like the National Endowment for Democracy (an arm of the CIA created to do in the open what the CIA did clandestinely).[52] This raises an interesting paradox I have previously explored: "how can anyone be a socialist if they genuinely think each time a socialist or communist party has been in power, it has resulted in great failures? What sort of arrogance is required to claim that everyone in the third world has failed at socialism, but we, the virtuous West, we are the ones who will succeed!"[53]

---

[51] Friedrich Engels, *MECW Vol. 27*, 227.
[52] Ben Norton and Marx Blumenthal, "DSA/Jacobin/Haymarket-sponsored 'Socialism' conference features US gov-funded regime-change activists," *The Grayzone* (July 06, 2019): https://thegrayzone.com/2019/07/06/dsa-jacobin-iso-socialism-conference-us-funded-regime-change/
[53] Carlos L. Garrido, "Examining the Gulf Between the Left and the Working Class in the US," *Midwestern Marx Institute for Marxist Theory and Political Analysis* (February 06, 2022):

This purity fetish position concerning socialist states is not only verifiably false, but revolutionary futile! Why would the working class follow something that has always failed? Especially since the working class under discussion has been generationally breastfed anti-communist propaganda. When workers ask the purity fetish Marxists: 'why would I organize for socialism if the media, schools, and my family have always told me that it leads to poverty, genocide, and societal failure?' what can the response of these 'socialists' be? Considering they themselves accept the same dishonest propaganda the workers have been force-fed to believe, it would look something like: 'yes, yes, that is all true; the problem is that those things in the real world called socialism were never actually socialism; socialism is really this beautiful idea that exists in its pure form in my head.' To accept struggling for socialism after that, the worker under discussion would have to be as infantile and simple-minded as the socialist he speaks to.

Instead of this, socialists and communists should be using the immense successes achieved by socialism in the Soviet Union, China, Cuba, Bolivia, etc. as examples for what socialism can achieve even while under the boot of constant hybrid warfare from the global imperialist system. We must be able to show our working class what socialism *has* provided for them, and what it *can* provide for us. Before this can be achieved, the left must be able to remove the dogmatic blinders which have given it a narrow, imperialist-friendly view of socialist and anti-imperialist states. They must be able to engage in a *concrete* study of past and present socialist experiments, to learn from their successes, and to understand their mistakes within their proper context, not in an abstract and ahistorical manner.

2- Rejection of 'Backward' Workers

In the context of the US, the purity fetish also manifests itself in the assessment of which parts of the working class are 'pure' enough to organize, and which must be left alone in fear of contamination. If a large chunk of the working class is socially conservative, and henceforth, fails to meet all the purity markers the enlightened PMC left has set as the a priori conditions for approval, they will be rejected as – in the words of

https://www.midwesternmarx.com/articles/examining-the-gulf-between-the-left-and-the-working-class-in-the-us-by-carlos-l-garrido

Hillary Clinton – a "basket of deplorables," or worse, as 'fascists' incapable of being brought to the socialist movement. For these Marxists the traditional communist slogan is no longer "workers and oppressed people of the world unite," it is "socially enlightened workers and oppressed people of the world unite." These 'Marxists' don't see in the millions of working class Americans who voted for Trump a group of people deceived by Trump's shallow and fake anti-establishment discourse; they don't see that what is implicit in that vote is a desire for something new, something which only the socialist movement, not Trump or any bourgeois party, could provide. Instead, they see in this large chunk of the working class a bunch of racists bringing forth a 'fascist' threat which can only be defeated by giving up on the class struggle and tailing the Democrats. Silly as it may sound, this policy dominates the contemporary communist movement in the U.S.

The purity fetish preeminent in Western Marxism forgets that, as Lenin said, one "can (and must) begin to build socialism, not with abstract human material, or with human material specially prepared by us, but with the human material bequeathed to us by capitalism."[54] Communists cannot pop into existence a 'pure' working class from the void, they must learn how to organize all workers irrespective of the differences the ruling class foists on the working masses to divide them. Communists must understand that the backwardness the working class may have will not be overcome if one ignores them – this will only lead them into the hands of the fascists, who are always a contending force in capitalism's moments of crisis. Instead, it must be acknowledged that only through class struggle can the most backward elements of the working class evolve. This does not mean you 'tail' behind them, but that you understand that because of their class position they are objectively revolutionary, and therefore, that their consciousness and emotions can always be elevated and rearticulated towards socialism. If communists do not have confidence in their ability to convince workers who don't already agree with them to struggle for socialism, how can they consider themselves communists? What are they doing besides preaching to the choir?[55] As Lenin eloquently noted,

---

[54] Lenin, *Collected Works Vol. 31*, 50.
[55] I'd like to thank my comrade James Befaunt from the Revolutionary Blackout Network, who brought up this analogy of preaching to the choir, lending a colorful image for this phenomenon, when he interviewed me in December 2022.

It would be an egregious folly to fear this "reactionism" or to try to evade or leap over it, for it would mean fearing that function of the proletarian vanguard which consists in training, educating, enlightening and drawing into the new life the most backward strata and masses of the working class and the peasantry. On the other hand, it would be a still graver error to postpone the achievement of the dictatorship of the proletariat until a time when there will not be a single worker with a narrow-minded craft outlook, or with craft and craft-union prejudices... The task devolving on Communists is to convince the backward elements, to work among them, and not to fence themselves off from them with artificial and childishly "Left" slogans.[56]

The purity fetish 'Marxists,' however, see the world statically and through an essentialist and idealist framework; they do not understand the struggle for socialism as a material process – to them the forces that exist currently will always remain where and as they are. This outlook is fundamentally antagonistic with the task bequeathed to communists by history; namely, to develop the subjective conditions for revolution. However, this outlook is not eternal; it too is subject to change and can be overcome through the development of the dialectical materialist worldview. When one consistently applies in their revolutionary practice the understanding that the world is "dominated by change and interconnection, and that if we study the world concretely, we may begin to decipher the forms and structures through which change and interconnection take place," the anti-dialectical essence of the purity fetish can be overcome.[57]

3-   Rejection of National Past

There is a second unique form the purity fetish takes in the US. Gramsci's work helps us understand that communists must appeal to the common sense understanding and feelings of the masses, and from there, critically rearticulate kernels towards socialism. If rejecting socialist experiments abroad and large chunks of the working class at home was not enough, the purity fetish Marxists add on to their futility in developing

---

[56] Lenin, *Collected Works Vol. 31*, 51.
[57] Garrido, *Marxism and the Dialectical Materialist Worldview: An Anthology of Classical Marxist Texts on Dialectical Materialism*, 51.

subjective conditions for revolution by completely disconnecting themselves from the traditions the American masses have come to accept. Bombastic and ultra-left slogans such as "Abolish America" have become more and more popular in American communist spaces. For them and their one-sided outlook, the U.S. is reducible to settler colonialism, imperialism, exploitation, slavery, and all the crimes of the ruling class and its state. Some have even gone as far as saying that white workers don't actually exist – that they're just 'settlers.' Since US history is not pure enough for their purity fetish outlook, it must be discarded wholesale. This is done through synecdochally treating the history of the owning class and its state as the whole history of America.

Paradoxically enough, although US history is too impure for contemporary US communists to accept, it was always praised by the leaders of the global communist movement, from Marx, to Lenin, to Mao, to Ho Chi Minh, and Fidel. For instance, in his 1918 'Letter to American Workers,' Lenin would say:

> The history of modern, civilised America opened with one of those *great, really liberating, really revolutionary wars* of which there have been so few compared to the vast number of wars of conquest which, like the present imperialist war, were caused by squabbles among kings, landowners or capitalists over the division of usurped lands or ill-gotten gains. That was the war the American people waged against *the British robbers who oppressed America and held her in colonial slavery*, in the same way as these "civilised" bloodsuckers are still oppressing and holding in colonial slavery hundreds of millions of people in India, Egypt, and all parts of the world…

> *The American people have a revolutionary tradition which has been adopted by the best representatives of the American proletariat*, who have repeatedly expressed their complete solidarity with us Bolsheviks. That tradition is the *war of liberation against the British in the eighteenth century and the Civil War in the nineteenth century*. In some respects, if we only take into consideration the "destruction" of some branches of industry and of the national economy, America in 1870 was behind 1860. But what a pedant, what an idiot would anyone be to deny on these grounds *the*

immense, world-historic, progressive and revolutionary signifi-cance of the American Civil War of 1863-65![58]

A century and a half after the American Declaration of Independence from the English crown, in 1945, Ho Chi Minh would quote its ideals in the Vietnamese Declaration of Independence from France and Japan, where he sums them up in the following manner: "All the peoples on the earth are equal from birth, all the peoples have a right to live, to be happy and free."[59] Almost a decade after, in 1953, Fidel Castro would quote this document at length in his eminent 'History Will Absolve Me' defense, following the assault on the Moncada barracks. A little more than a decade after, Mao Tse-Tung would say in a 1965 interview with American journalist Edgar Snow that the US

> Had first fought a progressive war of independence from British imperialism, and then fought a civil war to establish a free labor market. Washington and Lincoln were progressive men of their time. When the United States first established a republic, it was hated and dreaded by all the crowned heads of Europe. That showed that the Americans were then revolutionaries.[60]

For all the undeniable and condemnable flaws of the ruling class's history, we must not forget that in the underbelly of this history lies its opposite – a long, arduous history of struggle against various forms of exploitation and oppression. This is the history of figures like Thomas Paine, Thomas Skidmore, John Brown, Frederick Douglass, August Willich, Daniel DeLeon, Eugene Debs, Bill Haywood, Elizabeth Flynn, William Foster, Henry Winston, W.E.B. DuBois, Martin Luther King, and thousands more. This is the history, further, of the abolitionist movement, of the workers movement, of the civil war and reconstruction period, of the suffrage movement, of the various socialist, communist, and anarchist organizations that emerged in the late 19th and early 20th century. This is the history, in essence, of the struggle against capital, the state, and the various

---

[58] V. I. Lenin, *CW Vol. 28* (Moscow: Progress Publishers, 1974), 62, 69.
[59] Ho Chi Minh, *Ho Chi Minh on Revolution: Selected Writings Vol. 3* (New York: New American Library, 1967), 141.
[60] Mao Tse-Tung, *Selected Works Vol. 9* (Peking: Foreign Language Publishers, 1994), 458.

tactics used to keep the working mass divided amongst race, sex, religion, and other factors which hinder the collective class struggle.

This is a history which should raise the spirits of today's communists with pride, letting us feel that the struggles we wage today continue the legacy of those who, for centuries, have fought the same fight in the same land. It should offer our struggles a new dimension of historical urgency, grounded on the commitment to not let struggles of previous generations of compatriots be in vain.

An honest glance at our history will help one recognize that the country has been composed of a unity of two opposed struggling poles – one which fights to defend the interests of the accumulation of capital, the other which seeks to defend the interests of working and oppressed peoples. These poles represent the political struggles of what Dr. Martin Luther King Jr. called the "two Americas" – one which is "perishing on a lonely island of poverty" in the "midst" of the other, which wallows in "a vast ocean of material prosperity."[61]

The history of those who have fought for socialism, peace, workers' rights, indigenous, black, and women's rights, is not a separate history which stands outside of America fighting against it. Instead, this history is an immanent extension of the injustices that have permeated our country. The workers who partook in these struggles, in their great majority, saw themselves as the real representatives of the American people and of the American values of life, liberty, pursuit of happiness, sovereignty, the right to revolution and to a government genuinely of, by, and for the people. They saw themselves as taking the progressive side of the 1776 revolutionary tradition forward, to socialism, which they considered to be its practical and logical conclusion. As the late historian Staughton Lynd wrote,

> For almost two hundred years all kinds of American radicals have traced their intellectual origins to the Declaration of Independence and to the Revolution it justified. They have stubbornly refused to surrender the memory of the American Revolution to

---

[61] Martin Luther King Jr. *The Radical King*, edited and introduced by Cornel West (Boston: Beacon Press, 2015), 237.

liberalism or reaction, insisting that only radicalism could make real the rhetoric of 1776.[62]

In *The Souls of Black Folk*, W. E. B. Du Bois (unquestionably one of the greatest American socialist theorists and literary writers – sometimes called the American Lenin) says that "there are to-day no truer exponents of the pure human spirit of the Declaration of Independence than the American Negroes."[63] Three decades after, in his *Black Reconstruction* – not only his magnus opus, but one of the most important books for understanding modern America – Du Bois would express a similar sentiment, saying that "democracy died save in the hearts of black folk."[64] In this text, Du Bois lucidly describes how the Civil War (or, America's second revolutionary war) was won thanks to the general strike of the black proletariat (i.e., southern slave), who fled north, and, in so doing, became "doubly valuable" for the union – as they both weakened the south by destroying its productive capabilities (i.e., the south lost the labor power of the black worker), and added strength to the north in the form of an added mass of black labor, soldiers, spies, etc.[65] This not only forced emancipation upon the north, but ultimately led to a dictatorship of labor in the south, spearheaded by the Freedman's Bureau and defended militarily by the federal government until the counterrevolution of property in 1876 (i.e., northern capital's betrayal of southern labor and alliance with the southern oligarchy).

This revolutionary movement towards a higher form of socialist democracy was understood by Du Bois – as well as by progressive figures of the time like Sumner, Stevens, Phillips, and Douglass – to be the genuine route that the American experiment should take to fulfill the ideals of the Declaration of Independence. It would entail not only the full realization, for the first time, of the ideals of 1776 in the world; but the

---

[62] Staughton Lynd. *Intellectual Origins of American Radicalism* (Cambridge: Harvard University Press, 1982), 7.

[63] Vijay Prashad, "Du Bois Before Lenin," *People's World* (November 2003): https://www.peoples-world.org/article/du-bois-before-lenin/ ; W. E. B. Du Bois, *The Souls of Black Folk*, in *Writings* (New York: The Library of American, 1986), 370. The 'American Lenin' is also how the Midwestern Marx Institute refers to Du Bois; see Noah Khrachvik, "The American Lenin - The Falsification and Reclaiming of Du Bois's Revolutionary Science in Modern America," *Midwestern Marx Institute* (March 2023): https://www.midwesternmarx.com/articles/the-american-lenin-the-falsification-and-reclaiming-of-du-boiss-revolutionary-science-in-modern-america-by-noah-khrachvik

[64] W. E. B. Du Bois, *Black Reconstruction* (New York: The Library of America, 2021), 40.

[65] Du Bois, *Black Reconstruction*, 99.

concretization of the ideals themselves, which would now have to account for questions of property, class, and race within the democratic creed of Jefferson and the Declaration of Independence. While socialists celebrate the Paris Commune every year as the first modern dictatorship of the proletariat, the fact that the dictatorships of labor in the reconstruction south are ignored – despite having arisen first (1865-1876), lasted almost a decade, and being much broader in scope – speaks volumes about the extent to which the ruling class has ignored and whitewashed our revolutionary history. In addition, it is also telling of the extent to which American socialists – let alone those of the rest of the world – have allowed the owners of capital to conceal such a tremendously important period of not only American or socialist history, but of world-history in general. The unearthing of this legacy, conjoined with the re-discovery of Du Bois, not just as some theorist, but as *the* father of American Marxism, is of utmost importance in overcoming the purity fetish and struggling for socialism in the U.S.

Herbert Aptheker, one of the leading American historians of the 20th century, an active militant in the Communist Party and editor of its theoretical journal, *Political Affairs*, expressed similar views in his celebrated text, *The American Revolution*:

> As the 18th century proceeded, a definite sense of American nationality appeared and developed; this encompassed all classes. The *desire for the right of self-determination* of this new nationality, which was at the *heart of the revolutionary effort*, was confined to no class, and most certainly was not a monopoly of the well-to-do. On the contrary, in the American Revolution, because of its nature, and because of the progressive character of the American bourgeoisie then, the active involvement of the masses of workers and farmers was notable. [The revolution had] an interrelated phenomenon – the progressive and democratic content of the effort attracted the masses; the participation of the masses helped guarantee and enhance the democratic content of the effort.[66]

---

[66] Herbert Aptheker, *The American Revolution: 1763-1783* (New York: International Publishers, 1960), 22.

William Z. Foster, one of the most cherished general secretaries of the Communist Party USA (1945-1957), and himself a laudable historian of progressive American history, wrote in his text, *The Negro People in American History*, that

> The Revolution beginning in 1776 was a bourgeois revolution, with strong democratic currents within it. It unified the nation and established American national independence, freed the national market from English domination, and opened the way to the more rapid development of trade and industry: it largely abolished the feudal land tenure system, separated Church and State, and set up a Republican form of government. The Revolution also created objective conditions for the realization of considerable political rights by the farmers and artisans: its greatest weakness was that it did not abolish Negro chattel slavery.[67]

When the French Revolution occurred in 1789, the most progressive and democratic actors in the American Revolution were fully behind it, while the most reactionary elements – the Hamiltonian Federalist ilk – urged their colleagues to go to war with France and red-baited (for the first time in US history) the Jeffersonian democrats, calling them "Anarchists, Communists, atheists, destroyers of the home, and paid agents of revolutionary France."[68] "But," as Foster writes,

> The vituperative attacks had little weight with the popular masses, who were then in an ascending revolutionary spirit. Consequently, in the elections of 1800 Jefferson won the presidency in one of the greatest popular demonstrations in the entire history of the United States. The people would not allow themselves to be robbed of the democratic fruits of the Revolution. Jefferson's Republican-Democratic victory was a victory for capitalism, as well as for democracy; *and in these times, inasmuch as it was developing the social forces of production, capitalism was a progressive social system.* Jefferson's cultivation of the poor farmers and small

---

[67] We must add the genocidal treatment of the native population as the other major 'weakness.' William Z. Foster, *The Negro People in American History* (New York: International Publishers, 1954), 50.
[68] Foster, *The Negro People in American History*, 58.

producers was the main means, indispensable at that time, to lay the broadest base under production in general, and also under American democracy. The policy of Hamilton and his Federalist camp, on the other hand, could only have resulted in the strengthening of reaction and of the existing feudal elements, the planters and their system of slavery. This would not have furthered industrialization, much less popular democracy.[69]

The early progressive elements of the Revolution were also concerning themselves, at such an embryonic stage in the development of capitalist relations, with inequalities of property ownership and its effects. Thomas Jefferson, for instance, understood that the "enormous inequality" in property relations was the cause of the "misery [of] the bulk of mankind," and that, as Herbert Aptheker notes, this concentration of capital was "the central threat to democratic rights."[70] In noticing how the interest of capital can turn a government of, by, and for the people into a government of, by, and for big business, Jefferson would go on to draw a distinction between the democratic man and the aristocratic man. The aristocratic man, he argued, "fear[s] and distrust the people, and wish[es] to draw all powers from them into the hands of the higher classes," which he labeled as those which own the "banking institutions and monied incorporations."[71] The democratic man, on the other hand, "identif[ies] with the people, ha[s] confidence in them, cherish[es] and consider[s] them as the honest and safe depository of the public interest."[72] Jefferson believed the aristocratic man, if he came to dominate the American government, would "destroy the freedoms" secured by the 1776 anti-colonial revolution.[73] He saw, as Noam Chomsky notes, an "obvious contradiction between democracy and capitalism."[74]

A similar observation, of course, was made by Thomas Paine – without a doubt the most progressive figure within the 'founding fathers.' In his 1795 *Agrarian Justice,* after seeing what the bourgeois democratic revolution accomplished in two decades, he would argue:

---

[69] Foster, *The Negro People in American History*, 58-59.

[70] Aptheker, *The American Revolution*, 105.

[71] "From Thomas Jefferson to Henry Lee, 10 August 1824," *Founders Online,* National Archives, https://founders.archives.gov/documents/Jefferson/98-01-02-4451.

[72] "From Thomas Jefferson to Henry Lee, 10 August 1824," *Founders Online.*

[73] Noam Chomsky, "Democracy and Education," *Counterpoints* 422, (2012): 60.

[74] Chomsky, "Democracy and Education."

> The present state of civilization is as odious as it is unjust. It is absolutely the opposite of what it should be, and it is necessary that a revolution should be made in it. The contrast of affluence and wretchedness continually meeting and offending the eye, is like dead and living bodies chained together.[75]

The first generation of home-grown socialists, flowering in the 1820s and 1830s, saw Jefferson's prediction actualize itself in the embryonic industrialization period of the US. In the face of growing inequalities and disparities, thinkers and activists like Langdon Byllesby, Cornelius Blatchley, William Maclure, Thomas Skidmore and others, developed the Jeffersonian ideals of the declaration of independence into socialism, what they considered to be its practical and logical conclusion.[76] Maclure, who is now remembered simply as the 'father of American geology,' collaborated with Robert Owen in constructing New Harmony, one of the first American utopian communist communities celebrated in a critical manner by Marx and Engels. In line with the assessment Jefferson and Paine made (presented above), Maclure would argue that "millions have not been practically free in any country or under any form of government, where they have been emancipated from physical oppression, by liberal theories."[77] The Jeffersonian democratic ideals would be unfulfilled within the context of capitalist relations of production. Socialism was required so that the progressive spirit of 1776 could be realized. The progressive side of the American revolution, in short, was the ideological embryo for the development of American socialism, and, in figures like Wendell Phillips, Fredrick Douglass, Charles Sumner, and Thaddeus Stevens, for the abolitionist movement.

The progressive parts of the early history of the country are not unproblematic with regards to issues of race and gender. This is true. As Domenico Losurdo has shown in his book, *Liberalism: A Counter-History*, the liberal revolutions and their theorists all contain a paradoxical "tangle of freedom and oppression," wherein the "twin birth" of anti-monarchist

---

[75] Thomas Paine, *Agrarian Justice*. In *The Thomas Paine Reader*, ed. Michael Foot and Isaac Kramnick (London: Penguin Classics, 1987), 482.
[76] David Harris, *Socialist Origins in the United States* (Netherlands: Van Gorcum & Company, 1966), 10.
[77] William Maclure, *Opinions on Various Subjects Vol. 1* (Nabu Press, 2011), 450.

liberal ideals arise conjointly with enslaving and genocidal practices.[78] This objective contradiction cannot be ignored. But we must keep two things in mind. The first, that all new things arrive not from the future, or unbidden from our minds, but from the past; that is, as Marxism teaches us, they develop out of what was and therefore carry with them parts of that past. The second, that out of the progressive elements of these processes developed movements which were better able to address issues where the early progressives fell short. From the Marxist perspective, what is considered 'progressive' within the lens of universal history is that which is able to move society forward, to usher in a new era of social relations with more advanced productive capabilities. It is undeniable that, in this sense at least, the American Revolution was a tremendously progressive event, symbolizing a nodal point beyond which a new era in world history would emerge.

In his short story, *Tres Héroes*, the Cuban philosopher, poet, and anti-colonial fighter, José Martí, would say the following about Simon Bolivar, Father Hidalgo, and San Martin:

> Their mistakes must be forgiven, because the good they did was greater than their faults. Men cannot be more perfect than the sun. The sun burns with the same light rays that warm us up. The sun has spots. Ungrateful men only talk about the spots. Grateful men talk about the light.[79]

American Marxists cannot allow their purity fetish to continue making them function as the 'ungrateful men' Martí critiques. As I have argued before,

> A similar, perhaps less forgiving, view can be held with respect to Thomas Jefferson [and the progressive traditions of 1776 in general]. Although nothing can erase his role as a slave master and leading figure in the US's genocide of native peoples, it is indubitable that his democratic and republican ideals served as the ideological ground for socialist, abolitionist, and other progressive

---

[78] Domenico Losurdo, *Liberalism: A Counter-History*, trans. Gregory Elliott (Brooklyn: Verso Books, 2014), 34, 37.
[79] José Martí, (1891), "Tres Héroes." In *Páginas Escogidas*, ed. Óscar Montoya (Bogotá: Editorial Norma, 1994), 41.

movements in the US. Just like the spots cannot be erased to emphasize the light, the light cannot be erased to emphasize the spots.[80]

The progressive and socialist struggles of our country's past were not 'Anti-American' or working under slogans such as "death to America." They saw the owning classes, their state, and the various bourgeois apparatuses as the real anti-Americans, as the ones who keep our population alienated, exploited, and oppressed while periodically sending them to wars abroad, where they lose limbs and lives fighting people whom they have more in common with than those who sent them to war. We must recall the words of the great Paul Robeson as he was being tried by the House Committee on Un-American Activities in 1956: "Jefferson could be sitting here, and Frederick Douglass could be sitting here, and Eugene Debs could be here."[81] And when he was asked about the patriotism of his friend, Ben Davis, a Communist Party leader and New York City councilmen, he said "I say that he is as patriotic an American as there can be, and you gentlemen belong with the Alien and Sedition Acts, and you are the nonpatriots, and you are the un-Americans, and you ought to be ashamed of yourselves."[82]

If this tradition is forgotten, we will be doing the owning classes a favor – for this is what they've done to our revolutionary tradition in the history books taught in our schools, where it has either been erased, sanitized, or domesticated. If we ignore this tradition because of its lack of purity, we tear the historical legs from the socialist movement and yield to what McCarthyism has been dishonestly propagandizing the American working masses to believe – namely, that socialism and communism are foreign and antagonistic to America. In addition, we would (as we currently are) rip ourselves off from establishing any connection with the masses and their common sense understanding and feelings.

No working class person will support a struggle which aims at bringing about the annihilation of their country. They would, however, support the sublation, i.e., the overcoming, of our present bourgeois state by a worker's

---

[80] Carlos L. Garrido, "John Dewey and the American Tradition of Socialist Democracy," *Dewey Studies* 6(2) (2022), 78.
[81] Paul Robeson, "Testimony of Paul Robeson before the House Committee on Un-American Activities, June 12, 1956," *History Matters* https://historymatters.gmu.edu/d/6440/
[82] Robeson, "Testimony."

state. This is how the communists of the past, guided by the dialectical materialist worldview, understood their connection to their history and their masses. The qualitative transformation involved in a revolution is not a full-fledged annihilation; something is always preserved and elevated into the new society. For American communists this has meant a fight to eliminate the evils of capitalism, imperialism, racism, sexism, and so on, while preserving and having pride in the history our people have in fighting against those exact evils. In the process of doing this, communists in generations past would lead the masses to understand, as the saying goes, that socialism is as American as apple pie! This is something that we can do again if we can overcome the purity fetish.

The Importance of Fighting National and Historical Nihilism

Historical and national nihilism can be cancer cells to the morale of any revolutionary movement. If left unchecked, it slowly grows and festers until it gets so large that it's too late to do anything about it, and it overwhelms and destroys the movement. In trying to understand and combat this cancer, it is an imperative that we remember the words of Georgi Dimitrov, a giant of the world communist movement, in his 1935 speech to the Seventh World Congress of the Communist International. Here he would say the following comments on *national nihilism,* a phenomenon rampant in Western Marxism today:

> Mussolini does his utmost to make capital for himself out of the heroic figure of Garibaldi. The French fascists bring to the fore as their heroine Joan of Arc. The American fascists appeal to the traditions of the American War of Independence, the traditions of Washington and Lincoln...
>
> Communists who suppose that all this has nothing to do with the cause of the working class, who do nothing to enlighten the masses on the past of their people in a historically correct fashion, in a genuinely Marxist-Leninist spirit, who do nothing *to link up the present struggle with the people's revolutionary traditions and past* -- voluntarily hand over to the fascist falsifiers all that is valuable in the historical past of the nation, so that the fascists may fool the masses.

No, Comrades, *we are concerned with every important ques-tion, not only of the present and the future, but also of the past of our own peoples*... We Communists are the *irreconcilable oppo-nents, in principle,* of bourgeois nationalism in all its forms. But *we are not supporters of national nihilism,* and should never act as such...

Comrades, proletarian internationalism must, so to speak, "ac-climatize itself" in each country in order to strike deep roots in its native land. *National forms* of the proletarian class struggle and of the labor movement in the individual countries are in no contra-diction to proletarian internationalism; on the contrary, it is pre-cisely in these forms that *the international interests of the prole-tariat* can be successfully defended.

It goes without saying that it is necessary *everywhere and on all occasions* to expose before the masses and prove to them con-cretely that the fascist bourgeoisie, on the pretext of defending general national interests, is conducting its selfish policy of op-pressing and exploiting its own people, as well as robbing and en-slaving other nations. But *we must not confine ourselves to this.* We must at the same time prove by the very struggle of the working class and the actions of the Communist Parties that the proletariat, in rising against every manner of bondage and national oppression, is the *only* true fighter for national freedom and the independence of the people.

The interests of the class struggle of the proletariat against its native exploiters and oppressors are not in contradiction to the in-terests of a free and happy future of the nation. On the contrary, the socialist revolution will signify *the salvation of the nation* and will open up to it the road to loftier heights. By the *very fact* of building at the present time its class organizations and consolidat-ing its positions, by the very fact of defending democratic rights and liberties against fascism, by the *very fact* of fighting for the overthrow of capitalism, the working class is fighting for the fu-ture of the nation.

The revolutionary proletariat is fighting to save the culture of the people, to liberate it from the shackles of decaying monopoly capitalism, from barbarous fascism, which is laying violent hands on it. *Only* the proletarian revolution can avert the destruction of

culture and raise it to its highest flowering as a truly national culture -- *national in form and socialist in content...*

If we act in this spirit, if in all our mass work we prove con-
vincingly that we are free of both national nihilism and bourgeois
nationalism, then and only then shall we be able to wage a really
successful struggle against the jingo demagogy of the fascists.

That is the reason why a correct and practical application of
the Leninist national policy is of such paramount importance. It
is *unquestionably an essential* preliminary condition for a successful struggle against chauvinism -- this main instrument of ideological influence of the fascists upon the masses.[83]

I have quoted this document at length because it magnificently captures
one of the central forms the purity fetish expresses itself through in the
US: *national nihilism*. We cannot allow the most reactionary segments of
our monopoly capitalist class to win the ideological war over the national
history of our people. We must be able to work creatively, to take the progressive elements of our national past – which, although obscured by our
ruling class, exist in abundance – and to rearticulate these elements towards socialism. This is what Dimitrov means when he says that we must
"enlighten the masses on the past of their people in a historically correct
fashion, in a genuinely Marxist-Leninist spirit."[84] National and historical
nihilism must be destroyed. As J.V. Stalin correctly said, "national nihilism only injures the cause of socialism, because it plays into the hands of
the bourgeois nationalists."[85] It is a quintessential manifestation of the purity fetish – because the national past is impure, the purity fetish Marxists
reject working with its progressive elements and incorporating these into
the struggle for socialism.

Our country's history, indeed, is a history marked by conquest, enslavement, genocide, exploitation, imperialism, and all the other evils
brought by the development of the capitalist era in world history. It is also
marked, however, by the struggles against feudal absolutism; by a promise
for universal life, liberty, and pursuit of happiness – all demands which
are unfulfillable within the capitalist mode of life; by the struggles against

---

[83] Georgi Dimitrov, *The United Front: The Struggle Against Fascism and War* (London: Lawrence and Wishart, 1938), 61-64.
[84] Dimitrov, *The United Front*, 62.
[85] J. V. Stalin, *Collected Works Vol. 4* (Moscow: Foreign Language Publishing House, 1953), 94.

chattel slavery, wage slavery, genocidal attacks on indigenous communities; by the struggles, in the 20th century, against fascism, imperialism, for civil rights, for peace, etc. This is a complex, heterogeneous, and impure history. It is, in short, a contradictory history, containing within itself a unity of opposing forces – one which fights for human emancipation, the other which fights for preserving the tyranny of capital. We must learn how to use these objective contradictions to our advantage. The task ahead of us requires aligning our struggles today with the positive elements of the past and connecting the moribund capitalist-imperialist forces of our day with our past's negative elements.

This is not an easy task. As Mao argued while condemning national nihilism,

> Every nation in the world has its own history and its own strengths and weaknesses. Since earliest times excellent things and rotten things have mingled together and accumulated over long periods. *To sort them out and distinguish the essence from the dregs is a very difficult task, but we must not reject history because of this difficulty. It is no good cutting ourselves off from history and abandoning our heritage. The common people would not approve.*[86]

This difficulty is embedded in the need to develop socialism according to the concrete conditions of a given country. As Lenin said: "All nations will move towards socialism; it is inevitable. But the process will not be exactly the same for all nations … each nation will have its own characteristics."[87] This is why, the same Lenin which in one breath condemns Russia's role as "a prison of nations," in another says:[88]

> Are we class-conscious Great-Russian proletarians impervious to the feeling of national pride? Certainly not. We love our language

---

[86] Mao Tse-Tung, "Chairman Mao's Talk to Music Workers," in *Selected Works of Mao Tse-Tung Vol. 7, Marxist Internet Archive*: https://www.marxists.org/reference/archive/mao/selected-works/volume-7/mswv7_469.htm

[87] V. I. Lenin, *Collected Works*, vol. 28. [In Chinese.] (Beijing: People's Publishing House, 1990). Cited in Hui Jiang, "The Great Contribution of the CPC to the World Socialist Movement over the Past Hundred Years," *International Critical Thought* 11(4) (2021): https://doi.org/10.1080/21598282.2022.1996836

[88] Lenin, *CW Vol. 20*, 219.

and our motherland; we, more than any other group, are working to raise its laboring masses (i.e., nine-tenths of its population) to the level of intelligent democrats and socialists. We, more than anybody are grieved to see and feel to what violence, oppression and mockery our beautiful motherland is being subjected by the tsarist hangmen, the nobles and the capitalists.

We are filled with national pride because of the knowledge that the Great-Russian nation, *too*, has created a revolutionary class, that it, too, has proved capable of giving humanity great examples of struggle for freedom and for socialism; that its contribution is not confined solely to great pogroms, numerous scaffolds, torture chambers, severe famines and abject servility before the priests, the tsars, the landowners and the capitalists.

We are filled with national pride, and therefore we *particularly* hate *our* slavish past... and our slavish present, in which the same landowners, aided by the capitalists, lead us into war to stifle Poland and the Ukraine, to throttle the democratic movement in Persia and in China, to strengthen the gang of Romanovs, Bobrinskis, Puriskeviches that cover with shame our Great-Russian national dignity.[89]

With details adjusted to context, we may say something similar about the US today. We, too, could say that we are proud of our revolutionary class and its rich revolutionary history. We, too, could say that precisely because we are proud of this history – and because we are driven by the "great feelings of love" for the people that Che mentions – we wholeheartedly condemn our genocidal, slavish, exploitative, and imperialist past and present.[90]

For Lenin, Mao, Fidel, Ho Chi Minh, Chávez, and other successful socialist leaders, the question they asked themselves concerning their national past was never "is it pure enough?" but "how can we organically use the national traditions ingrained in our people's common sense and feelings to fight for socialism?" In China this has taken the form of Socialism with Chinese Characteristics; in Cuba this has meant incorporating José Martí and the anti-colonial traditions into socialist construction; in

---

[89] Lenin, *CW Vol. 21*, 103-104.
[90] Ernesto Guevara, *Che Guevara Reader* (New York: Ocean Press, 2003), 225.

Venezuela this has taken the form of Bolivarian socialism; in Bolivia this has taken the form of combining Marxism (scientific socialism) with indigenous communistic traditions which have been around for centuries. The same can be seen in the socialist struggles in Africa (Pan-African Socialism), the Middle East (Islamic Socialism), and other parts of Asia and Latin America. One would have to be blinded by a *liberal tinted American exceptionalism* to think that the struggle for socialism in the US will itself not have to follow this concrete universal tendency seen around the world, where scientific socialism functions as the content which takes form (i.e., concretizes) according to the unique circumstances in which it is being developed.

Dialectics (both in Hegel and in Marxism) rejects the idea of an unchanging, pure, ahistorical universal, and instead explains how universals are necessarily tied to historically conditioned concrete particulars. Universals are always concrete – that is, they can only exist and take their form through the particular. "The universal," as Hegel and Lenin emphasized, "embraces within itself the wealth of the particular."[91] There is no such thing as abstract socialism. Socialism is the universal which cannot exist unless concretized through the particular. Socialism in the US will have to take form in accordance with the unique history and conditions of the country. By embracing a petty historical and national nihilism, the contemporary Western Marxists find themselves unfit to 1- understand their national past concretely (i.e., dialectically and correctly) and 2- build a successful struggle for socialism. This infantilism is a manifestation of the purity fetish and will be removed when such an outlook is overcome by the dialectical materialist worldview.

Few people have studied the counterrevolution in the Soviet Union closer than the Chinese, who are keen on not repeating the same mistakes as the Soviets. One of the most important lessons the Chinese take from the fall of the USSR is precisely the existential importance of rejecting historical nihilism (*lishi xuwuzhuyi*), which they describe as the view that "Marxism was outdated and socialism had 'failed' (after 1989 in Eastern Europe and the Soviet Union); the CPC was an aberration in Chinese history; fawning on foreign powers; and the denial of or 'farewell' to the revolution."[92] As Roland Boer has noted, "the disaster that befell the Soviet

---

[91] Hegel, *Science of Logic*, 58.
[92] Roland Boer, *Socialism with Chinese Characteristics: A Guide for Foreigners* (Singapore: Springer, 2021), 93.

Union is seen as a clear example of the effects of historical nihilism."[93] As Xi Jinping has argued,

> [One] important reason for the disintegration of the Soviet Union and the collapse of the CPSU is the complete denial of the history of the Soviet Union, and the history of the CPSU, the denial of Lenin and other leading personalities, and *historical nihilism confused the people's thoughts.*[94]

Unlike in the USSR, as Carlos Martinez notes,

> Although the Chinese leadership made serious criticisms of certain policies associated with Mao (in particular the Great Leap Forward and the Cultural Revolution), it has never come anywhere close to repudiating Mao and undermining the basic ideological and historical foundations of Chinese socialism. No Chinese Wall has been constructed between the Mao-era and the post-Mao era; the two phases are inextricably linked.[95]

As Deng Xiaoping said in 1980:

> We will forever keep Chairman Mao's portrait on Tiananmen Gate as a symbol of our country, and we will always remember him as a founder of our Party and state ... We will not do to Chairman Mao what Khrushchev did to Stalin.[96]

Although these comments are specifically made within the context of socialist states, the universal we can observe concretized in the particular is the general condemnation of historical nihilism. Historical and national nihilism share a common logic – a rejection of the past because of its impurity. If the past contains errors, excesses, imperfections, it is *nothing*. Only that which is pure is salvageable. This manifestation of the purity

---

[93] Boer, *Socialism with Chinese Characteristics*, 10.
[94] *The China Questions: Critical Insights into a Rising Power*, edited by Jennifer Rudolph and Michael Szonyi (Cambridge: Harvard University Press, 2018), 23.
[95] Carlos Martinez, *No Great Wall*, 54.
[96] Deng Xiaoping, "Answers to the Italian Journalist Oriana Fallaci," *The Selected Works of Deng Xiaoping* (August 1980): https://dengxiaopingworks.wordpress.com/?s=Answers+to+the+Italian+Journalist+Oriana+Fallaci&submit=

fetish not only prevents a correct dialectical assessment of the past, but also works as a deadly fetter for the movement towards socialism. In the US, historical and national nihilism are not simply attitudes about the past – they are attitudes about the present and future. Their relevance is far from being merely scholarly. If we are unable to connect our people's progressive history to our contemporary struggle for socialism, and understand the U.S. and its history as a social totality riddled, like all things, in objective contradictions, then socialism will be forever in the realm of a pure idea, unachievable and out of reach. The battle against historical and national nihilism is one we must win if we want any chance at winning the class war.

Conclusion

The flaws of Western Marxism cannot be easily reduced to a gap in how we think about the different temporalities of 'communism.' Although this is indubitably an important factor, it is one which is included within the more concrete, and hence, integrative, concept of the purity fetish. With the lens of the purity fetish, we can capture the multiple forms in which Western Marxism falls into anti-dialectical positions in their analysis of the world, often making it politically conservative, anti-communist, and even reactionary at times. With this concept, we are better equipped to comprehensively understand how the variety of 'errors' and 'futilities' found in Western Marxism are interconnected and ideologically grounded on a Western philosophical tradition which considers truth to be on the side of the pure, abstract, static, and homogeneous. Instead of attacking Western Marxism's failures in a disconnected and piecemeal manner, when armed with an understanding of the purity fetish, we can address these obstacles at their root – in the worldview they, whether consciously or not, use to approach the world.

In the context of the U.S., this gives us the capacity to see how questions like: whether a country's socialist or anti-imperialist struggle should be supported; or whether a portion of the less 'enlightened' working class can be organized; or whether the national past should be blanketly condemned, are not at all disconnected, as may appear on the surface, but are instead assessed through the same metric, namely, whether they measure up to the 'pure' idea of what socialism, the working class, or national history should be. This is a modern form of socialist utopianism. It divorces itself from the contradictory character of the world and from the fact that the new never fully rids itself of the old but reincorporates parts of it in a more developed form. Like Zeno, when the Western Marxist approaches the contradiction between their ideal of pure socialism in their mind and the reality of socialism in the present, they consider it impossible that the impure reality they see is socialism. This utopianism is an integral component of Western Marxism's purity fetish. Therefore, it can be considered reactionary from the standpoint of it returning to a pre-scientific (i.e., Marxist) form of socialism.

Further, in going beyond Losurdo's bridge of temporalities thesis, we can observe how the purity fetish outlook is materially grounded on a variety of objective forces: 1) the PMC composition of the 'left;' 2) the role imperialist state departments and capitalist foundations play in funding and proliferating this 'compatible' anti-communist 'left;' and 3) the role that the iron triangle of academia, the media, and NGOs play in ensuring that the PMC 'left' is embedded in the culture, ideas, and customs of the institutions where such a compatible anti-communist Marxism is promoted, effectively creating a condition where the spaces this 'left' creates for socialist organizing are anathema for working class people. Overcoming the purity fetish, therefore, requires a self-conscious critique and change of the objective forces that ground Western (and U.S.) Marxism's poverty of outlook.

Contemporary U.S. society is showing all the signs of a *comprehensive crisis*, with objectively revolutionary conditions expected only to intensify in the near future. These conditions provide fertile soil for a revolutionary transformation. However, objective conditions are not enough. It is necessary for the subjective factor (i.e., the masses' development of socialist consciousness with the aid of a revolutionary vanguard) to develop into revolutionary organs of power grounded in the working class. In the U.S., the purity fetish, which overwhelmingly dominates the outlook of most communist organizations, presents a fetter for the actualization of this subjective factor. Only by overcoming this outlook can the subjective conditions for revolution develop, and hence, can social revolution genuinely be put on the table.

This requires, however, three processes to occur. These processes should not be thought of separately, but dialectically; the development in one simultaneously brings forth the development in another.

> 1- A process of critical self-reflection by the dominant socialist and communist organizations of the U.S. These must become aware of their class composition, and how the influence of the iron triangle of academia, the media, and NGOs have come to ground their political culture and their purity fetish outlook.
>
> 2- Once critical self-awareness has occurred, all efforts should be made to have the working class – not the PMC - become the center and soul of the organizations.
>
> 3- Theoretical education must become one of, if not *the*, central priority. Every cadre should master and be able to consistently approach the world through the dialectical materialist worldview.

This *cannot* be reduced to the dogmatic memorization of a few slogans and conclusions which are then copied and pasted from one context to another. To have a genuine transformation of outlook, to be able to approach the world through a dialectical materialist framework, is a creative and complex endeavor; one which requires the constant concrete study of the concrete.

The purity fetish is all around us. It seeps into our pours and poisons the air we breathe, driving the working class away as sure as any plague. If we are to fight our ruling class, if we are to emancipate ourselves from the chains of capital, if we are to fulfill the historical role set down in Marx and Engels, then we must overcome the purity fetish. This is how we carry the living spirit of Marxism-Leninism into our age and overcome the one-sided extremes of right-opportunism and ultra-leftism, which are but various forms through which the purity fetish manifests itself.

Index

Printed in Great Britain
by Amazon

20801024R00071